An
Almost
Chosen
People

An Almost Chosen People

| The Moral Aspirations of Americans |

Editors | Walter Nicgorski
Ronald Weber

The University of Notre Dame Press
Notre Dame   London

The middle portion of I. Bernard Cohen's article is based, to some degree,
on his earlier publication *Science and American Society in the First Century
of the Republic* (Columbus: Ohio State University, 1961).

Library of Congress Cataloging in Publication Data
Main entry under title:

An Almost chosen people.

    Essays originally delivered at a Bicentennial
conference held at the University of Notre Dame in the
spring of 1976; sponsored by the University of Notre
Dame and Saint Mary's College.
    1. United States—Civilization—Congresses.
2. United States—Moral conditions—Congresses.
I. Weber, Ronald. II. Nicgorski, Walter. III. Notre
Dame, Ind. University. IV. Saint Mary's College,
Notre Dame, Ind.

E169.1.A47183   973   76-41343
ISBN 0-268-00581-8

Contents

Contributors

MARSHALL SMELSER, Professor of History at the University of Notre Dame, is the author of several works in American history, including *The Democratic Republic, 1801-1815* and *The Winning of Independence*.

MARTIN DIAMOND, Professor of Political Science at Northern Illinois University, recently completed a year's fellowship at the National Humanities Institute at Yale. He has published extensively on the political theory of the Founding Fathers.

SYDNEY E. AHLSTROM, of Yale University, is one of the country's leading scholars in the field of American religious and intellectual history. His book *A Religious History of the American People* won a National Book Award in 1973.

ALFRED KAZIN is well known as a writer and literary critic. His most recent book about American literature and culture is *Bright Book of Life*.

I. BERNARD COHEN, of Harvard University, is one of the nation's leading figures in the field of the history of science. He is currently at work on a book entitled *Science and the American Republic*.

PETER L. BERGER, Professor of Sociology at Rutgers University, is head of the Eastern Sociological Society and an associate editor of *Worldview*. He is the author of six books, the latest of which is *Pyramids of Sacrifice—Political Ethics and Social Change*.

VINCENT HARDING, Director of the Institute of the Black World in
Atlanta, was recently Visiting Professor of Afro-American
Studies at the University of Pennsylvania. The recipient of a
Danforth-Harbison award for outstanding teaching in 1970, he
has written and lectured widely on racial issues in American
society.

THEODORE M. HESBURGH, President of the University of Notre
Dame, is chairman of the Overseas Development Council, a
Washington-based private organization promoting the interests
of the underdeveloped nations, and serves as trustee of the
Rockefeller Foundation. He is the author of *The Humane Im-
perative: A Challenge for the Year 2,000.*

WALTER NICGORSKI is Associate Professor in the General Program
of Liberal Studies at Notre Dame.

RONALD WEBER is Director of the Program in American Studies at
Notre Dame.

Foreword

The eight essays that follow originally were delivered as papers at a bicentennial conference held at the University of Notre Dame in the spring of 1976 and entitled "An Almost Chosen People: The Moral Aspirations of Americans." The conference was sponsored by the University of Notre Dame and Saint Mary's College.

The conference ought to provide a forum for reflection on America as a moral drama, in the past as well as now. It is commonly said that America is not a people or a geographic entity so much as a moral idea, a spiritual hope, a dream of the spirit. Throughout our history, from Massachusetts Bay through Vietnam and Watergate, the feeling has persisted—intense at times, perhaps faint now—that the hope America holds out is grounded not so much in material prosperity as in moral attainment. In turning to this story the conference was turning to the deepest levels of inner history in America—a story of failed vision as well as noble vision, of virtue realized and unrealized.

President Lincoln's description of Americans as an "almost chosen people" seemed to fittingly characterize the direction of the conference both in its evocation of the idea of moral specialness in America and its ironic and paradoxical rejection of the idea. In its latter sense Lincoln's phrase also seemed to capture the contemporary air of skepticism and gloom that often attaches to discussions of American moral aspirations. These are among the matters we wish to take up briefly in the Afterword.

The speakers were asked to address the conference theme from the vantage point of their academic specialties and professional experience. They responded, as expected, variously. Some engaged the theme of moral aspiration and the American notion of chosenness very directly, others by examining ideas and historical developments only broadly—though no less importantly—directed to the subject. Some responded with familiar scholarly detachment, others with candid personal feeling. But whatever the varieties in approach as well as subject, the essays stand as commentaries in the bicentennial year on one of the oldest conceptions of America—as a spiritual experiment, a voyage in goodness as well as power, perfection as well as progress.

ix

The contributors to the conference and to this volume were selected from suggestions offered by the faculties of the University of Notre Dame and Saint Mary's College. The editors are grateful for the special assistance in selection given by a committee composed of Professor Elizabeth Noel of Saint Mary's College and Professors Michael J. Crowe, J. Philip Gleason and William P. Sexton of the University of Notre Dame.

The editors wish to thank Professor Thomas Stritch, editor of the *Review of Politics* published at the University of Notre Dame, for his assistance in preparing the essays for publication in the July, 1976, issue of the journal. The editors wish to acknowledge the overall guidance and support offered by Dr. Thomas P. Bergin, Dean of the Center for Continuing Education at Notre Dame, and also wish to acknowledge the partial underwriting of the conference by the Indiana Arts Commission and the Indiana Committee on the Humanities in cooperation with the National Endowment for the Humanities.

W.N.
R.W.

An
Almost
Chosen
People

An Understanding of the American Revolution

Marshall Smelser

The study of the American Revolution probably loses something because we know how it came out, which may lead to creating interpretations unknown to the revolutionaries. Nevertheless, if we keep in mind the danger of finding omens to fit our prejudices, we may profit from a reappraisal aimed at better understanding.

I

The Anglo-Americans seem always to have been fitting themselves for independence. Let us first sum up the preconditions which inclined them temperamentally to rebellion. No matter how far back one looks, the white Anglo-American lacked meekness. By the middle of the seventeenth century, Massachusetts, the first colony able to subsist alone, prepared to defend its charter forcibly against the King, said the loss of its charter would cancel its allegiance, claimed that neither statute nor royal writ could cross the ocean, and announced neutrality in the English Great Rebellion. Economic independence had stiffened necks.

In the 1730's and 1740's a religious movement, the Great Awakening, stirred hundreds of thousands and incidentally strengthened their tendency to do their own political thinking. It was not like a modern revival, but more resembled the very moving civil rights and peace demonstrations of the 1960's. Preachers' emphasis on the binding power of divine law over conscience convinced converts they must act for their own salvation and not obediently trust their destinies to anointed rulers.

The Anglo-Americans were violent. From the seventeenth century through 1775 there were eighty-four furious riots.

Beginning in the 1680's the British colonies were caught up in four world wars. Expanding royal government, to make itself more powerful, tried to direct the colonials more minutely in the imperial interest. The self-satisfied colonials resisted through their elected assemblies and began to see their royal governors in the same harsh

3

colors that seventeenth-century Englishmen had painted the royal Stuarts.

As the colonies grew explosively, they became so rich that Britain saw them as necessary to her strength. As early as the 1740's the British began to assert control more vigorously, and in exasperating ways, although foreign wars postponed a showdown. The American Revolution might have come earlier except that wars with France kept interrupting British plans to do the things that would make the Americans angry enough to rebel.

Long before the 1760's, local American grandees quarreled with imperial officials stationed in America about the wisdom of royal policies, whether on seaborne trade, on military quotas, on Indian policy, or on crown lands. Perhaps the Anglo-Americans *should* have been grateful for subsidies, markets, and naval protection, but they preferred to attack governors with eighteenth-century vituperation and to oppose policy with the rhetoric of the seventeenth century. British officials began to be bored by American claims to know how to run an empire better. After a few more years of acid exchanges, moderate views were no longer acceptable to strong minds on either side of the Atlantic.

The British eventually tired of edicts and persuasion. The stable and confident North Ministry answered American riots and tumults with statutes (now called Coercive or Intolerable Acts) to remove any constitutional barriers to the use of force to compel obedience to imperial policy. With hindsight we can see this as imprudent. By drawing the sword Britain did what earlier could not have been done: the shocked Americans united in the Continental Congress, a body intended at first as a protest group, but which, in time, became a government to enforce disloyalty to Britain as patriotism in America.

A stiff-necked, violent, inner-directed people were convinced that a dimly known Britain was harassing them. They resolved that creeping imperialism should creep no farther. They had all the temperamental qualities needed for independence well before 1776.

II

What made the Americans so upset?

It is natural to think that large results must have complex causes. Sometimes the story of the American Revolution is overcomplicated by this assumption. There is a large literature which tries to explain—stormy polemics of the revolutionary period and contradictory explanations by today's historians—which we can only hurry past. Perhaps the Anglo-colonials should have been content. No national population in the world had as high a standard of living (especially in diet) or as cheap a government, and they had a capital growth rate of about 2 percent, which is very high for a developing country. But British policy roused discontent.

Britain had its own problems, the most pressing of which was that five-eighths of public revenue went for interest on the very large national debt arising from the wars. For Britain's benefit the energetic Parliament decided to reshape the jerry-built imperial administration and to use it effectively to get revenue from America.

There was nothing maternal in Britannia's purpose. Surviving official memoranda of 1763 show a chilly, even antagonistic, determination to rank the Anglo-Americans below Britons in every way. While the colonials claimed their assemblies were little parliaments, the British classed them with borough councils. Americans, the British said, were virtually represented by the British Parliament where every member represented every subject of the King. Americans could not accept that because they clung to a medieval notion of a representative as a kind of personal attorney. On the other hand, if the Americans could arrange to be under the King alone, the Parliament would have seen it as an unwelcome enlargement of the King's power. Thus, stubborn Anglo-American elites in their petty provincial assemblies, accustomed to managing their own internal affairs, including taxes, saw every new British policy as a weakening of the Americans' only real power, the purse power.

There were other American material interests. Because of the extinction of French rule as far west as the Mississippi, Britain had new problems: clashing colonial claims to wild lands, protection of the Indians, the tempering of the excesses of the squalid fur business. The central authority could solve such problems, but separate provinces could not. Colonial magnates had dreamed of vast land speculations in the west, but a Royal proclamation of 1763 thwarted them by barring the westward movement of whites. Again, in 1774, all land northwest of the Ohio was made part of Quebec, where English-speaking land developers had no clout. Predictably, land speculators were among the leaders of the Revolution.

When the British attacked the problem of costs, they decided to make the Anglo-Americans pay for a large part of the standing army (to be kept, threateningly, in America), to levy American customs and internal taxes, and to make the Americans pay for their administration. The colonials had a reasonable fear that the number and kinds of taxes would rapidly multiply. They had been grudgingly paying trivial regulatory taxes, but without admitting their lawfulness. In fact, their representative bodies had always denied parliamentary authority to tax America. The British legal reply was to ask the Americans to *prove* their tax exemption. We can see the political issue: if the British Parliament could make Americans pay, no governor would ever again need local appropriations and each would be able to do without a colonial legislature. And, regardless of the legal merits of the British case, any policy which provoked such anger and outrage in profitable colonies was an unwise policy.

Britain insultingly gave the enforcement of these tax laws to Vice Admiralty courts, on the ground that American juries would not convict Americans. Vice Admiralty proceedings had neither grand nor petty juries. The judges privately examined defendants who were incriminated by anonymous informers. In England, defendants in such cases still had common law protections. Anglo-Americans concluded that the Parliament saw them as something inferior to Englishmen.

Americans also mistrusted Britain for ecclesiastical and moral reasons. Evangelical Protestants always feared the imposition of Anglican bishops. Worse, British behavior seemed evidence of the same papistical, absolutist corruption they had fought in the recent long wars with France. George III was beginning to seem as benighted and tyrannical as a Bourbon.

Even so, despite American opposition, the reorganization of the empire might have come off as planned if managed by wise men, but the character of the British Ministry and its servants in America worked to irritate rather than to mollify. American working people and the British soldiery despised each other. British army officers showed contempt for the colonial middle class. Royal Navy seamen behaved like pirates, while their captains impressed young men who had influential friends. Customs officers now found it harder to cheat the crown and turned to extorting from the merchants. A fourth of the new American revenue went to make soft jobs for friends of government. Governors filled their councils with flexible toadies instead of respected local leaders. And, while few Americans really understood English politics, the Ministry in Britain had a reputation as a group of unprincipled, power-hungry grafters.

In fairness, one should note that the colonial assemblies were as hungry for power as their British counterpart. Further, it is doubtful that the Anglo-Americans could have prospered from their legal monopolies of tobacco, indigo and furs in British markets without protection from the Royal Navy, for which they paid nothing, directly. On one side, the colonial leaders stood stubbornly against yielding their power and their standing in America. On the other, it was psychologically impossible for Britain to invent some new kind of imperial relationship. In the whole Christian era there was no precedent for the British to follow.

The intervention of the Parliament in colonial business made the crown seem alien. The habit of obedience was broken. Between American politicians defending English liberty as it ought to be, and British politicians defending English law as it really was, the two sides had taken positions from which they could not back down without shame. To the most energetic Americans the dangers from Britain began to seem greater than the risks of war. In their minds only two alternatives remained: the extinction of self-government in America, or separation from Britain. A wiser government might have led the Anglo-Americans, but no one could push them. A wiser government might have used the political skill of the Anglo-Americans, guided them, encouraged them, made them feel at home in the empire. But wisdom was in short supply in Britain.

III

Most Americans chose rebellion or loyalism in the 1770's. Except for a few conspicuous leaders, we are not sure why some became rebels and others became loyalists.* We are sure it was not a class war. There were social grades, but the richness of America and the ease of moving about ruled out class conflict among whites in most places. In the south, slave labor gave rich whites leisure for politics, supporting English rights on African wrongs. In the north the magnates resisted early; if there was to be resistance they wished

---

* One can suggest a very tentative psychological hypothesis: rebels venerated abstract ideals — virtue, duty, the common good — above friends and blood ties. Loyalists' codes were personal, clannish, placing highest values on families and friends.

to control it. When violence followed, most drew back in alarm, but others felt committed and stayed. In any event, the rebels were a majority, were skilled in self-government, and knew how to bring a majority to action.

Some writers have tried to rank leading rebels according to their zeal but each risked everything, since it is a legal maxim that in treason all accessories are principals. Nineteenth-century writers also wasted effort by describing the Revolution as one in which all people of learning, refinement, and conservative inclinations could take part. Only quiet palace revolutions meet that standard, and this was no palace revolution. Nevertheless we cannot equate men like Washington, Adams, and Jefferson with Robespierre, Lenin, or Hitler. Almost all of the rebel leaders were the leaders of local governments before the Revolution.

Space will not allow a roll call of leaders, but we must glance briefly at the person who did most to win independence and make it solid: George Washington. He was sturdy, cool, and usually just, but prone to blame others for his failures. The only thing he lacked in this world was higher status. The Revolution brought him that. The Revolution probably cost him $150,000, but he secretly liked becoming chief of state of a republic.

The rank and file behind these leaders came in the beginning from the seaport mobs which erupted off and on after the 1740's. They differed from the numerous contemporary English mobs only in comprising half a dozen nationalities and a dozen religions. All kinds of homegrown lower-class organizations—militia companies, volunteer fire companies, mechanics' clubs—later added to the numbers. The violence began in the towns. When war spread to the farmlands, where almost everybody lived, the rebels came from those who feared British novelties, and who would rather get along with old familiar courts and have old neighbors as public officials. There is nothing necessarily noble in the aims of these embattled farmers. It was just that they had workable homespun politics which they had mastered. Royalizing would diminish their part. Britain had become a foreign country to these heterogeneous, multiplying people.

American loyalist leaders, regardless of origins, wished to preserve the notion of a hierarchical society, but social standing was not grounded on royal support in America as it was in Britain. Some royal officials in America thought poorly of British policies in the

1760's, but could not take the leadership of change, since the British government never used the American patronage to build American political machines. Thus, the top royalists were ornamental personages, or the cousins of personages, but not true leaders. Active leadership fell to those most respected locally, the members of the boisterous and talkative assemblies in which Americans felt so much at ease. (Loyalists sometimes called England "home," which suggests that they did not feel at home in America.)

The worst British mistake of the Revolution was to overestimate the strength of loyalism. It was official policy to count half of the Anglo-Americans as loyalists, who needed only military help to regain power. The most recent careful reckoning concludes that loyalists were less than a fifth of the white population. In the north, loyalists were passive, or huddled behind the British army. Only south of Virginia were they vigorous. There, where warring partisans lived by looting each other, the War of Independence was atrociously waged on both sides. In all provinces loyalist property was seized and sold to the rich, both as punishment and to finance the war. About seventy thousand loyalists emigrated permanently.

British leadership did not sparkle. The King's ministers were not wicked, but were either distracted or ignorant. An aristocracy of fewer than two hundred families held all the seats in the House of Lords and could affect the election of most of the Commons. They held power by pedigree, by land monopoly, and by an iron penal code. At their head was prosy King George III, neither mad nor particularly bright, who used the British political system as well as any other politician. He was a party boss whose strength came from patronage. His circle of friends thought of the rebel Americans as naughty children, which was a serious misjudgment. The Ministry should have made contingency plans at least by 1774, but even members partial to America, like Edmund Burke and William Pitt, saw no theoretical limit on the powers of Parliament which "virtually" represented Americans.* British yielding would have been of grace only, not of right.

Only thirteen of thirty-three American colonies revolted. The seventeenth-century English theories of the rebels failed to persuade the Canadians to join; Nova Scotia and Florida were subsidized

---

* Virtual representation would seem fair if the members of the Parliament paid the taxes they levied on America and said the money came from America by virtual taxation.

garrisons, wholly dependent on Britain for money. White West Indians sympathized with the continentals, but were outnumbered ten to one by slaves, lacked local patriotism, and needed British force to maintain their little police states. In North America, the Revolution began in the self-conscious, self-governing, cosmopolitan five towns whose leaders were unwilling to defer longer to power so far away.

IV

The military story must not be separated from the rest of it. It has been fashionable in our lifetime to minimize military studies. In a republic such ignorance could be suicidal, since most republics have ended in military dictatorships.

The native force at the disposal of the rebels was the Continental Army.* The British army did not frighten Americans. Indeed, at first the Americans mistakenly thought the American militia was as good. They were ignorantly overconfident, but without overconfidence there would have been no Revolution. When they learned how hard it was going to be, they were in too deep to quit. As a loose league of equals the states ran a very poorly organized war. The civilian administration of supply and finance was a mishmash of improvisations, rather like a prom committee. The Congress was only strong in voting large paper armies, but that had a good effect because the British could not be *sure* they would never appear. The shabbily treated rebel troops won many well-fought small actions and few large battles, which shows their chief weaknesses were in transport and supply. If the military men had been in charge they might have run a disciplined Prussian kind of war, but the rebels always intended to prevent the United States from becoming a new Prussia.

The most important single ingredient of the military victory was the temperament of George Washington. His sturdy character made up for his lack of brilliance and panache. As a seasoned Virginia politician he knew how to keep the favor of the Congress. As a strong-willed Potomac valley baron he was stubborn enough to stay on duty continuously for eight years. As a soldier taking charge of sixteen times as many men as he had ever before commanded he

---

* We must look away from the navy, which lost all but one of its ships, and was a waste of time, money, and lives.

used his post for on-the-job training.

Opposed to the Continentals was a professional army with mostly amateur officers who did not know the useful tactical lessons learned in previous American wars. The Indians generally sided with the British for they had nothing to gain from a farmers' republic. Loyalists were less help than expected, because fewer, and because conservers are usually less lively than rebels. The British supply system was theoretically better than the rebels', but had difficulties in the interior where four out of five whites were indifferent or unfriendly.

One can list twenty-eight important battles (no two such lists would be identical), of which two were indecisive, thirteen were British victories, and thirteen American. All told, there were not more than five thousand combat deaths, but there were tens of thousands of prisoners taken. The British could have won in 1777, but not later—a fact it took four years to learn. After Yorktown, a battle not decisive in itself, the Ministry had to pay 20 percent for money borrowed in London. That was the end. It is worth noting that Yorktown was won by a prior French naval victory off Chesapeake Bay (a small battle) which made it impossible for the British army to leave by sea. Thus, this was a war fought on land but won on water.

The rebels could not suppy enough arms and gunpowder. The solution was an alliance with France, which cared nothing for the Americans but wished revenge against Britain. The French were self-servingly generous to the rebels. While expecting no gratitude, they spent more than twice as much for American independence as the Americans spent. The first big shipment of munitions made possible the victory over Burgoyne, even before the alliance. Some help came from the Dutch and from Spain (as help to France). Tsarina Catherine of Russia made a gesture at protecting neutral shipping from the Royal Navy.

The rebels still had ancient suspicions of the French. Clergymen saw the alliance with a Catholic monarchy as one more evidence of the mystery of God's ways. After France came openly into the war, in 1778, Britain was in grave trouble. Every important Atlantic seafaring nation was an enemy or an unfriendly neutral. That alone is almost enough to explain the result.

Britain had offered peace at frequent intervals from the start. The wary "one-issue" rebels always refused to talk unless Britain

recognized independence or withdrew its forces. Although unde-
feated and still powerful, Britain quit the war after Yorktown out
of sheer frustration. In Paris the American envoys, John Adams,
Benjamin Franklin, and John Jay, negotiated a splendid treaty, not
because they were moral superiors but because they were more capable. They secured independence from Britain without making the
United States a French satellite. At home there was no great peace
celebration. It was just as well, for this was not an end but a
beginning.

Why did Britain fail? There were both political and military
reasons.

To put down a revolution without brutality (and the British
were not brutal) requires reforms which please the rebels without
alienating the contented. This takes more skill than found in the
small pool of British talent. Lord Frederick North, the King's chosen
political agent, was not stupid, but he was lazy and distracted by
other matters. The King himself was not inspired or inspiring. As
an unknown versifier put it:

> George III
> Ought never to have occurred.
> One can only wonder
> At so grotesque a blunder.

The military was unable to invent novel solutions to the problems of a people's war of a kind unknown to British experience.
Always the Ministry overestimated the loyalists although they did
nothing to build their spirit. Naval strategy was poor compared
with British naval strategy in the other Anglo-French wars. The
entry of France diverted British energy to saving the West Indies,
which were valued more than North America. Finally, British
military leaders in America proved torpid or inept or even neurot-
ically disabled.

These reasons have served to explain the British loss, but are all
on one side. After all, *somebody* won.

Why did the American rebels win? Their military victory has
stirred wonder ever since. Some have seen it as the work of God,
but there are some persuasive natural reasons.

The members of the Congress, wiser than the British expected,
were at least as competent as the members of the Parliament. They

had long experience at self-government. After 1774, there were no loyalist members, which left the Congress free to talk of means instead of quarreling about ends. The combination of the Congress indoors and Washington in the field became unbeatable. The rebels ably used propaganda to appeal to settled convictions drawn from the Old Testament, classical history, and the Protestant Reformation. American propaganda won the contest for public loyalty.

The Anglo-colonials had a tradition of violence. Beginning in 1645, there were eighteen attempts to overturn colonial governments, six of them by violence. Indian or international war had been endemic. Mob action had been common, especially in the seaports. It was not out of character to use violence against royal government.

Unlike some other rebels, they were constructive. They were not out to destroy an old regime but to preserve what they thought was an acceptable older order.

They had French help which they needed to win in the way they won. But even before the French alliance the task of the British was hard, as shown by British military difficulties through 1777. To win, the British army had to destroy the Continental Army. The Continental Army had only to survive. Unless the Continentals surrendered or deserted in a body, it is hard to see how royal government could have been restored.

V

Let us turn now to what the successful Americans constructed. At home they built thirteen workable state governments. The builders were not levelers or democrats, but powerful men suspicious of powerful executives. Out of antagonism toward the idea of monarchy, the Americans made strong legislatures with figurehead governors, believing that the legislature, as the whole people, would rarely be despotic. To their new state constitutions they appended glorious bills of rights which they then ignored. (There *may* be a case of a state law ruled invalid by a state supreme court because against a state bill of rights, but one does not come to mind.) These state governments were built to win home rule for thirteen separate states, and no scruples stood in their way.

The Congress published a Declaration of Independence. We should clearly distinguish between what they meant in 1776 and what their statement means today.

To the publishers the Declaration was an episode of their diplomatic practice. They hoped for a French alliance. Alliances are made between independent states, hence they needed to declare their independence to the world. They included an appeal to natural law principles, since the positive law did not support them. Then they added a rejection of the King and a certificate of their existence. Today the moral aphorisms of the natural law draw the most attention, especially the clause that "all men are created equal," but in 1776 the Congress was making a very specific political point: we Americans are equal to those legalistic British. They were not calling on the world to join a moral struggle, as, for example, ᵗhe French revolutionaries tried to rouse all mankind. The natural law principles were not applied universally, nor even to American society by a Congress which included slave owners and slave traders. The constitutional and ratifying conventions, and the Federalist Papers, did not use the Declaration. Even Thomas Jefferson did not think it followed the flag to the Louisiana Purchase.

In our generation, people use the Declaration to attack colonialism. Obviously, it has taken on a broader meaning. This broadening began with the slavery quarrel, in which the equality clause was very useful. In the Lincoln-Douglas debates, Douglas construed the Declaration historically in a sorry cause and lost in the end. Lincoln construed it philosophically in a better cause and ultimately won the minds of the people through the Gettysburg Address, which made the Declaration the moral basis of the republic.

The revolutionary generation was a transmission belt for a public morality which had often been expressed before 1492. Any excellence of the moral aspirations depends in no way upon their immediate narrow utility to the Congress in 1776, but Americans have since accepted their wider application.

The Congress organized a loose league under Articles of Confederation. Posterity has called the Confederation feeble, chiefly because of the public scorn of those who wished to replace it with the Federal Constitution, but its leaders lacked experience in building a national government. The Confederation did some useful work. They won the war and won the peace, prepared the organization of the west, and guaranteed to pay the national debt, someday. The Congress also barred slavery from the Old Northwest, although it was perhaps not so much to limit slavery as to reserve the Northwest for white people.

Those leaders who had interstate interests knew the states had a tendency to fly apart. The departure of imperial government left a vacuum of power, and the Confederation never filled the vacuum. Even before peace, there was a movement to nationalize the confederated states. Brief tumults in the 1780's give the emotional force necessary to bring people to do what was needed to strengthen the system.

The strength-giving instrument was, of course, the Constitution of the United States, a venerated paper with, so far, enough strength to hold the nation together.

Its authors had different aims but harmonized well. One or another wished a common market, a taxing power to pay the debt, access to foreign markets by treaties, a force to protect independence in the international jungle, a guard for civil liberties. Being skilled republican politicians they caucused at Philadelphia and put everything in one charter. When they differed it was not on philosophy but on structure. If they had theoretical differences the states-rights people would have left, for it was plain they were framing a nation, not a league.

They transferred just enough power from the state legislatures to make a workable nation which could prevent mob rule or dictatorship. They drew on past usage and recent experience. (The result did not impress the doctrinaires of Europe.) The authors had to overcome American opponents who resembled our modern "radical right" and others who liked the notion of thirteen independent states without asking whether the country could survive as a cluster of new world Switzerlands.

The Constitution has become a sacred testament, from a natural tendency to glorify those who lived earlier. As for its divine perfection, hundreds of thousands have died in war because of certain ambiguities. It was not an exercise of philosophical brilliance. It was a successful working paper to meet specific needs of the 1780's.*

The Revolution also had a cosmetic effect, by hiding an oppression. The Constitution accepted slavery as a fact of life. The authors were not hypocrites, but were blinded by their centuries-old heritage of English racism. They not only did not abolish slavery,

---

* Financially it was a real bargain. The cost of the Constitutional Convention to the public was $1165.90, about $12,000 in 1976 dollars, hardly enough to stage a local bicentennial commemoration.

but entered an era in which free blacks were to be treated more harshly and slavery more firmly fixed. Because blacks were invisible, Philip Freneau, a democratic poet, could praise men for dying for freedom in a state which surely would have chosen King George before abolition. Blacks noticed the irony, and those who could left with the British evacuation, more than three thousand from New York alone.

It is convenient here to list some undeniable changes caused by the Revolution.

—It fixed the form of government as republican, and distributed the sovereign attributes of the King among the whole people.

—It planted some seeds of democracy, such as the popular election of lower houses, the absence of property and religious tests for federal office, the prohibition of titles of nobility, and the payment of salaries to officials.

—The free white Americans reached a consensus that they should struggle for what was due them, rather than accept public unpleasantness with resignation.

—Violence proved to be a useful and popular way to change public policy.

—Nationalism became stronger than provincialism.

—Perhaps because of the prevalence of lawyers among the leaders, the Revolution preserved the common law, despite early misgivings.

There is no social revolution in that brief list. Anatole France said of the French Revolution that wooden shoes went up the stairs as velvet slippers came down. Not so in America. Nor did the Revolution resemble recent anti-imperial wars, since there was no ethnic antagonism in a group of white Protestant males fighting other white Protestant males to ratify the status they had gained before the war. There were incidental social changes in America but they were not uniquely American. They were part of the social revolution of the west, beginning around 1500.

Organized religion had ebbed between the flood tides of the Great Awakening and the Great Revival of the nineteenth century. One might use the word "heathen" to describe the revolutionary generation. David Ramsay, a reflective rebel, said the Revolution had immediate bad moral effects—a failure of courts, a weakened sense of obligation, and a derangement of public worship.

Most of the several hundred leading American revolutionaries believed in an impersonal God and an afterlife, but considered theology outside of respectable learning. Their hope was to improve the world through logic, in which they trusted more than any Americans before or since. God's function was to give them enough intellectual power to get along without Him. They resembled neither the ancient Stoics, whom they admired, nor convinced Christians. To their credit, they were—grudgingly—tolerant of Jews and Catholics. Aldous Huxley wrote a limerick which applies here:

There was an old man of Moldavia
Who did not believe in the Savior,
    So he founded instead,
    With himself at the head,
The cult of decorous behavior.

The Founding Fathers were mostly of the Moldavian Rite.

But the Revolution was itself a revival. It made republicanism into a religion. The republic became the established church. As for faith and morals in the eighteenth century, one may sum up this way: the intellectual spokesmen of America in 1740 were clergymen, in 1790, lawyers.

VI

The American Revolution was staged by reluctant rebels for limited goals, which were well within their reach. It was a mild revolution compared to, say, the French and Russian revolutions. Almost all of the American heroes died in bed. They did not set out, foredoomed, marching to Utopia. They were less violent, less disruptive, less passionate than their modern European counterparts. They achieved a sober, almost inevitable, almost prosy revolution. Lacking ancient misty founding fables on the order of Romulus and Remus, modern Americans must make do with a well-documented story of practical political success.

A recapitulation is a proper conclusion here.

—The Anglo-American colonial people were prone to violence and were psychologically ready for disobedience long before the Revolution.

—They rebelled, not against heavy taxes nor loss of personal liberties, but against British policies, long in the making, which weakened the ability of local governments to ignore or resist Parliamentary changes in the standing order.

—The fact that a mere fifth of the white population stood fast in loyalty is a measure of the alienation of the Americans, or, to put it another way, a measure of the failure of British ministries actively to cultivate loyalty in America.

—The British forces were technically unable to win a war against a people on the far side of the ocean who were largely hostile or indifferent to traditional claims on their loyalty and who had the help of a naval power with a generous purse.

—The leaders of the American Revolution, while disagreeing on some matters, had no internal split on the main goal of independence and thus were able to lead the struggle from start to finish, and to build a civil society strong enough to preserve that independence.

—They justified their disobedience of the positive law by appeals to natural law, phrased very well, which later generations have honored, dignified, even glorified, as comprising the testament of American ideals.

The Idea of Equality:
The View from the Founding
Martin Diamond

Every age seems to have some dominating central idea, and every particular political system surely has some dominating central idea from which radiate all the institutions, processes, and the texture of life in that country. As Tocqueville long ago said, the dominating idea of our age, and of our political order in particular, is the idea of equality. Equality is therefore at once for us the source of our political benefits and also the source of our defects and dangers. That is to say, every dominating idea is the one that determines for the society its likeliest and greatest benefits and dangers, because the central idea is the one that can do the greatest and most pervasive good and by the same token also the greatest harm. Equality is for us that central principle, the one we have to grapple with and wrest good from, and likewise the principle from which come our greatest dangers. Equality is the political problem for mankind in the present age.

Tocqueville dates the movement toward modern equality from as early as the thirteenth century. Be that as it may, surely by the seventeenth century the question of equality was palpably forcing itself onto the agenda of Western civilization. It has fallen to America to be that country which had first fully to confront the question, to be that country the very existence of which is a kind of continuous confrontation of the question, and to be that country which, in my judgment, best teaches the world the way, in the circumstances of modernity, to reap the benefits equality yields and to avoid its faults and perils. It is our moral mission, so to speak, to teach, by example and political thought, and by our strength, a prudent posture toward modern equality and democracy.

This teaching is what Tocqueville was seeking when he chose to study and visit America. He selected America for two reasons. First, because equality having "come to the fullest and most peaceful completion" in America, it could there be most thoroughly investigated. He came because he hoped to find in America "the shape of democracy itself . . . its inclinations, character, prejudices and passions: I wanted to understand it so as at least to know what we

19

have to fear or hope therefrom" *(Democracy in America)*. And
second, he studied America because of her success in avoiding what
could be feared from equality: where, he asked, could one hope
for more "valuable lessons" on how to avoid the danger of "democratic tyranny" and achieve instead "democratic liberty"? It is with
Tocqueville's concern to secure in the age of equality what there is
to "hope therefrom" that we turn now directly to our topic.

The problem of equality dominated the decade of our founding.
The problem of equality dominates and darkens our lives now two
centuries later. And those two centuries of American existence may
be said to have been a two-century-long testing of the way the
American Founders sought to cope with the problem of equality.
Perhaps nothing, then, is more important for the purpose of our
national self-understanding than to reconsider the American posture toward equality as seen from the perspective of the Founding.

I

The view of the founding decade to be presented here, and of
the American posture toward equality and democracy therein revealed, will be made clearer if we are reminded first of the conventional academic wisdom on the subject. The dominant interpretation of the Founding during the last half-century is the view that
was developed and popularized by J. Allen Smith, Charles A.
Beard, and Vernon L. Parrington. Despite their differences, all
three agreed that the Framers had been retrograde with respect to
democracy. Their motives had been economically selfish and their
intention was to turn back the clock. They wanted to stop the
march to democracy allegedly so well begun during the Revolution
and so eloquently expressed in Jefferson's Declaration of Independence. This dominant academic view of the retrograde, un-
democratic intention of the Framers had two important corollary
views: first, that the Constitution established a fundamentally un-
democratic, or at best quasi-democratic, political system; second,
that this system gradually became democratized, or at least somewhat more democratic, by means of a series of democratic "break-
throughs." As taught by this school, American history reads like a
series of happy subversions of the original founding intention —
first by Jefferson, then Jackson, then Lincoln, then Roosevelt and
Wilson, then FDR, etc. Those who held this view should perhaps

have wondered what made the original Constitution so accommodatingly vulnerable. Perhaps they should have seen something thoroughly democratic there right from the beginning, and thereby would have understood our history better, namely, as the unfolding and testing of an original posture toward democracy rather than as a transformation to democracy from something opposed to it.

Not to see American history as such an unfolding and testing of the original principles on the basis of which America coped with equality is to obscure what is uniquely instructive about the American experience. And this is precisely the effect of the conventional academic view. By seeing American history as the sporadic overcoming of an antidemocratic Constitution, the conventional view converts the American experience from that paradigmatic experiment in democratic liberty which Tocqueville saw here into a mere uninstructive evolution of democracy.

Against this conventional view, I propose one that is nearly its exact opposite, one which restores to the American experience its instructive relevance to the problem of modern equality. To begin with, the Declaration of Independence must be placed in the right light. It was *not* a democratic document, as it has come to be understood by contemporary scholarship and even largely in popular understanding. To adapt Lincoln's phrase, we may say that the Declaration was "conceived in liberty and dedicated to the proposition that all men are created equal." That is to say, the Declaration teaches that the deepest stratum of American political life is the liberty in which it was conceived, and the proposition regarding equality teaches further that all men are created equally entitled to that liberty. In the spirit of John Locke, the Declaration became for Americans — and again we may use Lincoln's words — "a standard maxim for free society." The Declaration placed at the very foundation of American political existence the idea of equal liberty. But it went no further than that. It did not pledge the new Union or the newly created states to the democratic form of government. Proclaiming only the goal of equal liberty, the Declaration left open to future decision the question of what the form of government should be. It remained, after a decade of experience and deliberation, for the Constitution to settle that matter. Thus, far from its being retrograde with respect to democracy, it was in the Constitution that the American people finally made their commitment to the democratic form of government. It was in the Constitution that they chose the democratic form as the means by which to secure the Declaration's equal liberty for themselves and their posterity. But as we shall see, from a proper consideration of the meaning and relationship of the Declaration and the Constitution, it was a sober and cautious commitment to the democratic form of government; and it was, therefore, a democratic government carefully safe-guarded and structured so as to enhance the excellences of democ-racy while guarding against its dangers and defects.

This view of the Declaration may seem startling to some be-cause two of its key phrases — "created equal" and "consent of the governed" — have been particularly misunderstood as a result of having been wrenched out of context. Written within the horizon of liberty of the founding generation, they have been understood in-stead within the horizon of egalitarian democracy to which later generations have tended. But in fact the Declaration does not mean by "equal" anything at all like the general human equality which so many now make their political goal and standard. Jefferson's original draft of the Declaration is especially illuminating in this respect. All men, Jefferson first wrote, "are created equal and independent," and from that "equal creation they derive rights inherent and inalienable." The word *independent* is especially in-structive; it refers to the condition of men in the state of nature, to their utter nonsubordination, in the state of nature, to each other or any common political sovereign. In fact, this famous passage of the Declaration, in both its original and final formulations, must be understood as dealing entirely with the question of the state of nature and with the movement from it into political society.

Social contract theory, in the Lockean form upon which the Declaration is based, teaches not equality as such, but only equal political liberty. The reasoning of the Declaration is as follows. Each man is equally born into the state of nature in a condition of absolute independence of every other man. That equal inde-pendence of each from all, as John Locke puts it, forms a "Title to perfect Freedom" for every man in the state of nature (*Two Trea-tises of Government*). It is this equal perfect freedom, which men leave behind them when they quit the state of nature, from which they derive their equal "unalienable rights" in civil society. The equality of the Declaration, then, consists solely in the equal entitle-ment of all to the rights which comprise political liberty, and nothing more. Thus Lincoln wisely interpreted the Declaration in his Springfield address of 1857: "The authors of that notable instrument . . . did not intend to declare all men equal *in all respects.* They did not mean to say all were equal in color, size, intellect, moral developments, or social capacity. They defined, with tolerable distinctness, in what respects they did consider all men created equal—equal in 'certain inalienable rights, among which are life, liberty, and the pursuit of happiness.' "

Now "to secure these rights," men quit the insecure state of nature, and "Governments are instituted among men, deriving their just powers from the *consent of the governed.*" Here we can now begin to see the unambiguous meaning of the other phrase in the Declaration that is so often misunderstood. It has been transformed to mean rule by the consent of majorities, that is, consent according to the procedures of the democratic form of government. But the Declaration does not say that consent is the means by which the government is to *operate;* it says that consent is necessary only to *institute* or *establish* the government. It does not prescribe that the people establish a democratic form of government, that is, one that regularly operates by means of their consent. Indeed, the Declaration says that they may organize government on "such principles" and in "such form" as they deem appropriate to secure their rights. In this, the Declaration was again simply following Locke, who said that when men consent "to joyn into and make one Society," they "might set up what form of Government they thought fit" *(Two Treatises).*

That the people are free to choose whatever form of government they think appropriate is further evidenced when the Declaration speaks of the people's right to undo tyrannical governments. The Declaration states that "whenever any Form of Government" becomes destructive of the rights it was intended to protect, the people have the right to "alter or to abolish it." Now by "any Form of Government," the Declaration emphatically includes — as any literate eighteenth-century reader would have understood — not only the democratic form, but also a mixed form, and the aristocratic and monarchic forms as well. The Declaration thus plainly acknowledges the legitimacy of all these forms so long as they have not become destructive of the people's rights. That is why, for example, the Declaration had to submit facts to a "candid world" to prove the British king guilty of a "long train of abuses." Tom Paine, by way of contrast, could dispose of King George more simply. Paine deemed George III unfit to rule simply because he was a *king* and kingly rule was for Paine ultimately illegitimate as such. The fact that George was a "Royal Brute" was only frosting on the cake; for Paine his being royal was sufficient warrant for deposing him. But the Declaration, on the contrary, is obliged to prove that George was indeed a brute. That is, the Declaration holds George III "unfit to be the ruler of a free people" not because he was a king, but because he was a *tyrannical* king. Had the British monarchy continued to secure to the colonists their rights, as it had prior to the long train of abuses, the colonists would not have been entitled to rebel. It was only the fact, according to the Declaration, that George had become a tyrannical king that supplied the warrant for revolution. In short, on the basis of the Declaration, the Americans would have had no grounds to dissolve the political bonds that connected them with the England of George I, or of George II, etc. No grounds, that is, unless a detailed indictment could have been drawn against them for the same sort of "long train of abuses" that justified the separation from the England of George III. Thus the Declaration supplies no warrant for revolution against monarchy as such. Indeed, it is certain that most of the signers of the Declaration would have agreed cheerfully that the English "mixed monarchy" had been, and perhaps for the English themselves still was, the best and freest government in the history of mankind.

The Declaration, then, strictly speaking, is neutral on the question of forms of government. Any form is legitimate, provided it secures equal freedom and is instituted by popular consent. But as to how to secure that freedom the Declaration, in its famous passage on the principles of government, is silent.

When we recognize this silence of the Declaration, we can begin to appreciate that the Constitution represents the American people's decision to secure their equal liberty under the democratic form of government. But it is a sober and cautious kind of democratic government and reflects a sober and cautious posture toward equality and democracy. The *sobriety* consists in this: democracy is made, not the *end* of government, but merely the governmental *means* for the securing of the true end, namely, the people's equal liberties. This subordination of democracy to liberty is the highest and most salutary commandment of the Declaration. In viewing all forms of government as merely instrumental to securing to the people their inalienable rights to "life, liberty, and the pursuit of happiness," the Declaration teaches Americans to view even their own democratic self-rule coolly as merely instrumental to the still higher end of liberty. Whatever criticisms may be made of liberty as a final end, is there not something salutary in this American teaching that all forms of rule must be subordinated to a higher standard? And is not the preservation of liberty as that "standard maxim'" still the surest means by which to prevent the "manly and legitimate passion for equality" from degenerating into "a debased taste for equality . . . which induces men to prefer equality in servitude to inequality in freedom" *(Democracy in America)?* The *caution* of the Constitution consists in the conviction that the democratic means, like all governmental means, are inherently unreliable; as much as any other form of government, democracy can betray the end of liberty for which it is intended, and hence the democratic means must be safeguarded, channeled, and moderated. The cautious American posture toward democracy reveals the American people's sensible self-doubt regarding themselves, and that self-doubt was built into their Constitution. This caution the Constitution derives not primarily from the Declaration but from a source common to both the Declaration and the Constitution. This is the "new science of politics" of which Locke was a leading representative, and to it we must now turn.

II

The sober and cautious American posture toward equality and democracy may strikingly be contrasted with the enthusiasm of Jacobin democratic thought and with the still greater enthusiasm of Marxism-Leninism. Jacobinism and Leninism are immoderate and incautious because, unlike the American view, they do not see in democracy merely a means toward the fulfillment of equal liberty, and a risky means at that. Rather, they absolutize democracy; they immoderately see in democracy and equality the end of human existence itself; or, incautiously, they believe that all the other human goods will be attained simply by the expansion of democracy and equality. Such Jacobin democrats, Leninist egalitarians, and other enthusiasts of equality find American democracy and the traditional American posture toward democracy too phlegmatic for their taste, so phlegmatic that they deny to it even the title of

democracy. Like Smith, Beard and Parrington, all enthusiasts of
equality are driven to deny to American democracy its bona fides.
They try to give their criticisms of American democracy a rhetorical
form which, in the modern age of equality, gives to their arguments
an unfair advantage. That is, they seek to represent themselves as
democrats in opposition to the American un-democrats, or as the
representatives of true democracy against America's halfhearted
and perverted democracy. But we must deny them this unfair
rhetorical advantage and insist instead that the issue is between two
rival conceptions of democracy: between sobriety and enthusiasm,
between caution and optimism; between the American constitutional democratic republic that channels and constrains its democracy and a rival idea of democracy that wishes it to be entirely untrammeled and more and more purely itself; in Tocqueville's terms,
between a modest "manly" equality of liberty and a "debased"
imperialistic claim to equality in all human realms.

To confront these differences more fully, we must turn to the
roots of the American sobriety and caution. On what philosophic
basis rests the American conviction that popular rule, like all forms
of rule, is subject to degeneracy, and is capable of folly and oppression? And upon what philosophic base rest the cautious means by
which the American republic seeks to regulate its democracy, to
guard against democratic defects and dangers? The answers to
these questions lie in the eruption of modern political philosophy
from the sixteenth through the eighteenth centuries, in the eruption
of what has often been called the "new science of politics." As will
be evident, I am deeply indebted here to the late Professor Leo
Strauss, whose instructive account of the "battle of the books,"
ancient and modern, has done so much to restore to our understanding the meaning of the modern enterprise. This new science
of politics, in the context of which the American Founding must
be understood, must itself be understood in contrast with the tradition of classical political thought from which it radically departed.
The ancients saw man as capable of reaching nearly to the divine
and took their bearings from the highest possibilities of human nature. While the ancients had no illusions about the capacity of *most*
men, they thought that every resource of the political art should be
employed to draw out and up the potential of the exceptional few.
Their very idea of human nature led classical thinkers to make the
preeminent political task the bringing toward completeness or per-

fection the relative few who were naturally capable of fulfilling their humanness. The classical idea of human nature is, as it were, aristocratic: all men are human but some are more so, and that is the crucial political fact. The modern idea of human nature is democratic: no difference among us can reach so far as to alter our naturally equal humanness, and *that* is the crucial fact.

But that strenuous and demanding ancient political art, the moderns charged, had been ineffective and excessive — that is, "utopian." Despite two millennia of such elevated teachings, man's estate had still not been relieved; greed and vainglory ruled under the guise of virtue or piety. The religious tyrannies and wars of the sixteenth and seventeenth centuries, it was thought, had climaxed two millennia of the failure of the traditional political science. What is more, the whole rigamarole had been unnecessary. It was in fact possible, the new science argued, to achieve, not the delusive heights at which the ancients aimed, but solid human decencies, by far more efficacious and, at the same time, far less excessive means. This great new claim rested upon a new and aggressively more "realistic" idea of human nature. The new science would take man as he actually *is,* would accept as primary in his nature the self-interestedness and passion displayed by all men everywhere and, precisely on that basis, would work out decent political solutions. This meant, as against ancient and medieval exhortation and compulsion of man to virtue, a lowering of the aims and expectations of politics. And it meant the achievement of these more modest aims by a shrewd, but perhaps coarse, reliance upon those natural human passions and interests.

This realistic view of human nature is the philosophic foundation of both the American Founders' soberly instrumental view of democracy and of their cautious concern to mitigate its defects. Their realism prevented them from absolutizing democracy and thus indulging in the utopian expectations characteristic of democratic enthusiasts; and it also supplied them with the institutional and other strategies for the cautious constraints they placed upon the democratic form of government. But, ironically, what also followed from this new and rather debunking view of human nature was not only their chariness regarding democracy, but a new and powerful case for democracy in the first place. The important thing to notice is that this realistic view of man is far more debunking regarding the claims or pretensions of the few than it is of the

many. Indeed, in important respects, the new science of politics
had a far higher opinion than ancient thought had of the capacities
of most men, and it emphatically gave a higher priority and saliency
to those qualities and concerns which all human beings share. Thus,
the new science of politics of the sixteenth through the eighteenth
centuries culminated in a teaching that paved the way simulta-
neously for democracy and for prudent constraints upon it.

    With this observation, we are now in a position to return to the
Declaration of Independence and qualify the observations made
earlier. It remains exactly and salutarily true that the Declaration
leaves Americans free to choose whatever "form of government"
they deem appropriate, and thus leaves them free not to choose the
democratic form. Nonetheless, in a crucial way, the Declaration
can be said to *popularize* the whole of political life. In this respect,
the Declaration is following the new science of politics, and that
of John Locke in particular. As noted earlier, while ancient
political thought took its bearing from the radical inequality of
human capacities, modern political thought takes its bearings from
those respects in which humans are more nearly equal, or denies
the political relevance of human inequality. Thus Aristotle, for
example, argued that the monarchical regime rested its just claims
upon the fact that some human beings were so remarkably superior
in moral and intellectual capacities that they ought *as of right* rule
over their fellow beings. The just basis for aristocratic government
was a similar claim made on behalf of the exceptional few. And
again in a somewhat similar way, the argument made in behalf of
the "mixed regime" was likewise based upon the just, or at least the
partially just, claims of both the *demos* and the oligarchs. In
Aristotle's understanding of the polity, or what we may con-
veniently call here the mixed regime, the oligarchs are entitled to
a share in rule because, albeit in a perverted way, they do represent
the claims of unequal human excellence; that is to say, their
superiority in wealth makes them represent, pervertedly, what
would be the true claim to rule of aristocracy. On the other hand,
the *demos* represent the just claim that equals should share equally
in all things; but their claim is likewise a perverted one, because the
demos think that equality of "free birth" constitutes an equality in
all respects.

    The crucial point is that the ancient typology of regimes or of
"forms of government" is a typology based upon the variety of

claims to rulership as of right. In contrast with this ancient typology, we can now see clearly what was meant by the assertion above that the new science of politics and the Declaration had a *popularizing* tendency. The Declaration does not recognize *any* of the old rival claims to rule *as of right*. The only legitimate claim to political power (in Locke's sense) is the equal consent of each, that is, popular sovereignty. All other claims to rule are rejected by the Declaration because they rest upon some assertion of unequal excellence—of superiority of wealth, priestly standing, wisdom, strength, etc. Now the Declaration does not deny that men may well be unequal in these respects and, indeed, in all such respects. But it denies that inequality in any respect constitutes an *entitlement to rule*. Political rule, for the Declaration, derives exclusively from the equal natural entitlement of all to the benefit of certain inalienable rights. Governments exist, it must be remembered, only for the equal securing of these rights. Now the people may well decide that, for their own benefit, it would be prudent and "appropriate" to organize their form of government as a monarchy, or aristocracy, or a mixed form. But the *reason* for such monarchy, aristocracy, or mixed regime, would now be entirely different from the reasons in the ancient tradition. The authority of the monarch, or the aristocrats, or the rulers under the mixed regime, would now simply be in the service of the people, in the service of securing to them their equal liberty. This popularizes the end for all forms of government. In the ancient view, the end or rationale of each of the different regimes differs in accordance with the various claims of unequal merit to rule. After the new science of politics and the Declaration, the end or rationale of all the forms of government is utility to popular liberty. In the old view, the "common good" was understood to include certain virtues or excellences which could be nurtured and made preeminent only by the rule of those who peculiarly and unequally possessed those excellences. Now the common good came to mean the protection of what all had in common. In the new view, the securing of those virtues or excellences forms no part of the end of "political power," and, consequently, the claim of unequal excellence loses its political relevance. Henceforward, the common good means the protection of what men really have in common, namely, an equal interest in securing their inalienable rights. Political systems as a whole, and institutions and processes within them, acquire their essential nature from the human ends they are calculated to serve. The reason for a form of political rule—its end and rationale—is the essential, the architectonic, part of that system of rule. Thus the change made by the new perspective of the Declaration of Independence is very great indeed: after the Declaration, *forms of government* remain distinct, their differences remain politically important, and the people may freely choose among them; but the gulf between *regimes* in the old style is narrowed by the underlying popularization.

We may examine the effects of this popularization by considering in further detail the changes wrought by the Declaration and the new science of politics in the traditional idea of the mixed regime. In Aristotle's understanding, for example, the two great practical demands or claims regarding rule were those of the few rich and the many poor. These demands had somehow to be dealt with or accommodated. As we saw, each of these demands came in the form of a partially just claim to rule. The mixed-regime strategy was to balance these two partially just claims, these two otherwise domineering social forces, against each other in a political system—e.g., patricians and plebeians, Lords and Commons, etc.— where each had an equal and mutually balancing share of the rule. The statesmanly task was so to balance the conflicting claims and forces that out of the balancing would emerge a more complete principle of justice than that embodied in the two partial claims of the oligarchs and the poor as such. In this perspective, statesmanship has a kind of dialectical task of drawing out of the two opposing opinions upon which the regime is based an idea of justice higher than that on either's side; statesmanship is here intended to give the citizens at once something less and more, something higher, than their own notions of their happiness were they free to pursue them.

Now, as has been emphasized, the Declaration of Independence leaves the people free to adopt the familiar mixed-regime form. But, nonetheless, very much is changed by the popularization of the end of government. If the people decide it is prudent to let oligarchs have a share in the government they institute, this is done without any notion of the oligarchs' right to rule in virtue of their wealth, or in virtue of any merit they may claim for themselves. The only reason, on the principles of the Declaration, for giving the oligarchs such a share is some principle of expediency—for example, the expediency for securing popular liberty of having one group or another balance off the popular element. But there would be no deliberate intention of introducing into the society, by means of the oligarchic element, any principle of justice contrary to that of equal popular liberty. On such a basis, there would still be oligarchs and mixed regimes, but only pallidly so in contrast with similar regimes where the end is a deliberate admixture of conflicting principles of justice. And there would be little if any notion of the statesmanly harmonizing of rival opinions into a higher whole; the function of statesmanship in such a mixed regime would remain primarily to achieve what is expedient for popular liberty. (Such a conception of the mixed regime opened the path to the wholly democratic strategies of the separation of powers and bicameralism; and it was along this path that events actually did move.) Similarly, if the people established a monarchical or aristocratic form, it would not be because, on some principle of distributive justice, the finest few were entitled to rule. Rather, it would be because the people prudentially decided to avail themselves of the services of the able few and to allow them to be the public servants of popular liberty. Indeed, the idea of public service rather than any idea of honor and distributive desert becomes the public morality; ancient virtue is narrowed down to the modern view of virtue as civic-spiritedness.

We may sum up these observations by dealing explicitly with what has only been implied thus far—with the difference between the old idea of a *regime* and the modern idea of a *form of government*. The latter term is foreign to ancient thought. Its invention lies in the modern making of equal liberty the single end for all forms of political power. This would have been inconceivable to ancient thought which regarded each different regime as having its own proper and unique end, indeed as being constituted by that end. The "ruling element" and the "end" of each regime *had* to form a unique pair in each regime; the end of each regime could be achieved *only* by its appropriate ruling element. But equal liberty, perhaps because it is not a particular conception of justice in the old sense, *is* capable of being served in a variety of ways, that is, by the variety of legitimate forms of government. The narrower function of governance on behalf of the single end of equal liberty *can* be performed in a variety of ways; but the broader idea of ruling in a regime can only be actualized upon radically hetero-

geneous principles of justice and the ruling elements appropriate
to them.

We must turn our attention back from the popularizing
tendency of the new science of politics to its "realism" because
it is from this that the American Founders derived their cautious
strategies respecting democracy. Like "every votary of freedom,"
Madison said in *Federalist* 39, the American Founders were determined to "rest all our political experiments on the capacity of
mankind for self-government." But they had no utopian expectations regarding that capacity. Unlike contemporary sanguine
egalitarianism, they did not expect that the mass of mankind could
ever rise to such levels of mind and character as would warrant the
untrammeled rule of the majority. They did not believe that such
a transformation of human nature could be effected by any means,
not by education, leisure, greater affluence, the experience of
political participation, the benevolent influence of collective social
arrangements, or any of the strategies upon which egalitarianism is
obliged to pin its hopes. On the contrary, they took for granted as
a fact of human nature the impossibility of finding wisdom and
virtue in sufficient quantities as to warrant, confidingly, the basing
of a democracy upon them. This is the harsh meaning of Madison's
statement in *Federalist* 51 recommending that the system of "opposite and rival interests" be made to substitute for the civic-
spiritedness that can never be sufficiently abundant to be relied
upon. Because of the perennial dearth of those qualities of mind
and character that could warrant "confidence"—an important
eighteenth-century term—in either the mass of men to be governed
or in those chosen to govern them, the American Founders regarded
an unrestrained democracy to be an invitation to disaster.

"If men were angels," Madison says in *Federalist* 51, "no government would be necessary," democratic or otherwise. And "if
angels [rather than human beings chosen by other human beings]
were to govern men, neither external nor internal controls on government would be necessary." Now not only are men not angels,
Madison clearly thought, but very few men even reached to the
level of the "better motives" that characterized the best men. And,
given the nature of things, that would always be the case. Thus
democracy had to be safeguarded against the natural human faults
intrinsic to it, whether from the people themselves in the form of
factious majorities, or from the usurpations of elected representa-

tives. Hence, while "a dependence on the people [i.e., majority rule] is, no doubt, the primary control on the government . . . experience has taught mankind the necessity of auxiliary precautions."

This is the foundation of all those cautious "auxiliary precautions" of the American constitutional system—the self-restraining, majority-restraining, principles and institutions of the Constitution, like the separation of powers, bicameralism, limited government, all the internal checks, etc. It is these which baffle and dismay all enthusiastic democrats, from Turgot and the Abbé Mably of the French Enlightenment, through Smith, Parrington, the later writers like Laski, and the numberless enthusiasts of our own time. They do not believe that democracy is in need of the constitutional fetters that we have imposed on ourselves, because they trust that democratic man will become, when some particular prescription or other is followed, the reliable citizen of the egalitarian future, of such excellence and mildness as to render unnecessary the arsenal of precautions the American Founders drew from the new science of politics.

Perhaps I can make clear the political significance of this disbelief in the necessity of precautionary restraints by relating a teaching experience that remains vivid in my memory. Quite a few years ago I was teaching a seminar at a European institution, the participants in which were midcareer administrative officials from many countries. I was arguing the case for Tocqueville and came under heavy fire from a South American Marxist-Leninist, as he described himself; he was from, it is important that I emphasize, a country not under communist rule. Pleasantly but very firmly, he denounced Tocqueville and all the American-style auxiliary precautions. His argument ran as follows: before the revolution, these institutional arrangements serve only to weaken the revolutionary forces and hamper their advance, and after the revolution such constraints are not necessary, because socialist democracy (not to say, the final stage of anarchy) would not need them; from a revolutionary perspective, then, these constraints were, first, positively harmful and, finally, useless. As we were arguing back and forth, I noticed on the other side of the room another seminar participant, an official from an Eastern European communist country, who was visibly quivering to get into the discussion. I got out of his way and he let fly. I *live* under communism, he said in effect, and I can tell you that these Tocquevillian strategies for the protection of liberty are desperately necessary, perhaps more than ever. It was an immensely telling argument, coming as it did with courage and anguish from a man living under the danger and with the problems, and addressed to a man who was cavalierly urging all mankind to take the fatal plunge.

This dramatic confrontation regarding the auxiliary precautions poignantly illustrated, in what I have been calling the rivalry of the two democracies, the issue between the self-doubting, self-restraining American constitutional democracy and the democracy of enthusiastic egalitarianism. The lessons of the twentieth century seem to me—as they did to my Eastern European student—to teach unqualifiedly the superior prudence of the American auxiliary precautions and of the sober and cautious posture toward democracy they express.

But the American posture is not simply a matter of cautiously constraining democracy. It consists also in a deliberate rejection of the claims of modern egalitarianism. We may conclude by considering that aspect of American equality which, ironically, deliberately presupposes and accepts the natural inequality of human capacities. Here we confront directly the issue of equality as it is disputed by the two democracies.

American democracy in the founding decade made, as we have seen, only a modest claim. It held men to be equal only in their equal right to "independence" in the state of nature and to political liberty in the civil state. John Locke was referred to earlier as the source of this view. Let us consider him more fully.

> 54. Though I have said above, Chap. II, *That all Men are by Nature equal,* I cannot be supposed to understand all sorts of *Equality: Age or Virtue* may give Men a just Precedency: *Excellency of Parts and Merit* may place others above the Common Level: *Birth* may subject some, and *Alliance* or *Benefits* others, to pay an Observance to those to whom Nature, Gratitude or other Respects may have made it due; and yet all this consists with the *Equality,* which all Men are in, in respect of Jurisdiction or Dominion one over another, which was the *Equality* I there spoke of, as proper to the Business in hand, being that *equal Right* that every Man hath, *to his Natural Freedom,* without being subjected to the Will or Authority of any other man (*The Second Treatise of Government*).

This is at the heart of the matter. Locke and the Declaration altered the long tradition of political thought in one decisive respect. They agreed with, say, Aristotle, that humans differ regarding "Excellency of Parts," and that "Virtue may give Men a just Precedency." But—and this is crucial—this inequality among men is *not* deemed great or significant enough to warrant the rule of the superior over the inferior as a matter of right. The "Precedency" warrants only voluntary, prudential, social approbation; it does not extend to political rule. Political rule is legitimate only when the people consent to it; no man is superior enough to rule another without that other's consent. In short, Locke and the new science of politics deny to human inequality the salient and intense force it was accorded in ancient and traditional thought. This has immense significance for American life which can only be barely suggested here. For example, the principle of equal entitlement to liberty, and the denial to inequality of its political authority, means that the ancient idea of distributive justice is publicly rejected. This surely has consequences for the deepest springs of action in society. Inequality balked of political reward will turn elsewhere, and excellence unelicited and unsupported by political reward may fail to fulfill itself. The denial no doubt has its costs.

But having acknowledged the alteration made by Locke in the political status of natural "Excellency," we must emphasize the other side of Locke and the Declaration, namely, that which limits equality to liberty and acknowledges human inequality in all other respects. Locke and the Declaration, and the political thought of the Constitution, presupposed that an inequality of virtue was rooted in human nature and that this inequality would manifest itself and flourish in the private, voluntary operations of society. The original American idea of equality and of constitutional democracy thus still deferred to a relatively high idea of virtue, despite the denial of its political claims. The American Founders understood this social flourishing to be the natural outcome of the combination of equal liberty and natural inequality. Because equal liberty meant that all had a roughly equal chance to exert themselves, unequal outcomes would inevitably result from the natural inequality of capacities.* In the Founders' understanding whoever says equality

---

* One example of this reasoning, as it applies to unequal property outcomes, is to be found in *Federalist* 10. From the protection by government of "different and unequal faculties of acquiring property, the possession of different degrees and kinds of property immediately results." Freedom to exert unequal capacities

of liberty thereby says inequality of outcomes; whoever says equality of outcomes thereby says inequality of liberty, because only the unequal handicapping of the superior will prevent their capacities from manifesting themselves.

Moreover, not only did the original American posture toward equality and democracy accept the social flourishing of inequality, but it was even the proud claim of Americans that their democracy would be the political system in which natural moral and mental superiority would in fact be justly rewarded by a discerning people. Here one only has to remember Jefferson's praise of the "natural aristocracy" and his most sanguine expectations regarding their probable place in American political life. Thus American democracy did not originally present itself as a political order in which a general equality would be achieved, but rather as that political order in which natural excellence rather than artificial privilege and pretense would most flourish. So little, then, was the original American idea of equality egalitarian in anything like the modern sense. Nothing, in my judgment, is more dangerous today than those subverting conceptions of human nature and justice which deny that there are men and women who deserve "Precedency" because of their virtue or excellence, or which would deny to American democracy its aspiration to be that political society which best defers to the deserving.

The issue, as the American Founders understood, was not how to extinguish inequality, but to decide how best to cope with it. Perhaps, then, we ought to alter the terms of the contemporary debate on equality. Indeed, the way the issue is now stated seems to me fundamentally false and gives away too much advantage to those who present themselves as the champions of modern equality. The issue is now debated as somehow a question of equality versus inequality. But if the Founders were right in believing, as nearly all of us somehow know however evasively we acknowledge it, that inequality really is ineradicably rooted in human nature, then it really is inextinguishable. In that case, the real question is not whether to seek to achieve equality as against inequality. The

---

necessarily results in unequal outcomes. This passage, by the way, is not protective of existing patterns of wealth distribution as it may appear to some contemporary readers. Madison is in fact concerned not to protect established wealth as such, but rather the process by which the "faculties" continuously receive their due outcome.

political questions before every political order are *how* to allow to inequality its ambit and, above all, *which* inequalities to let flourish. Which to depress and how? Which to nurture or high-tone, and how? Which to crush and how? If you close the door, inequality will come in the window. If you close the windows, it will seep through the cracks.

Since inequality will inevitably find some way to manifest itself, perhaps modern egalitarianism, which pretends to extinguish inequality, is in fact simply the shield and slogan of the cunning who will rule in the name of equality. Perhaps it is the shield behind which some kinds of unequal capacities—say those of a certain kind of intelligentsia, or demagogues, or bureaucrats—advance their interests at the cost of other unequal capacities, perhaps more socially useful or morally superior.* If the authentic political question is not a matter of equality versus inequality, but of which pattern of inequality to cause to prevail, then the language of contemporary political debate should be altered. The decisive question, then, is whether American democracy has shown how best to tame inequality, or whether the regimes that call themselves egalitarian hold out a greater promise of mildness in this regard. In such a debate between the two democracies, we have little to fear. In American equal liberty and constitutional democracy we have a resource within our past and within ourselves with which to answer boldly the contemporary aggressions of that "debased taste for equality . . . which induces men to prefer equality in servitude to inequality in freedom."

---

* Both Irving Kristol and Peter Berger have recently suggested shrewdly that the intellectual champions of egalitarianism may well have, or think themselves to have, quite material stakes in the movement toward egalitarianism.

The Religious Dimensions of American Aspirations

Sydney E. Ahlstrom

A topic like moral aspiration raises questions that no historian can long neglect if he deals with sovereign national entities such as the United States. One of the most challenging questions to be faced has to do with those mysterious bonds of affection and loyalty that provide whatever degree of psychic unity and collective aspirations a country may possess. In responding to a question about the *religious* dimension of national aspirations, however, I am tempted by the promise of a shortcut modeled on an argument that gained prominence among nineteenth-century Baptists belonging to the Landmark movement who, despite the absence of clear historical evidence, wished to establish the unbroken continuity of the Baptist succession from apostolic times to the present day. It took the form of a syllogism:

> God has promised never to leave the world without a witness to Christian truth; Baptist churches are the only true churches; Therefore the Baptist succession is unbroken.

In a similar but even more expeditious manner the main question before us could be solved at a stroke by a simple assertion: all aspirations are by their very nature religious. Nothing reveals the ultimate concern of an individual more clearly than his or her aspirations; indeed, this proposition occupies a very central place in my own efforts to write a religious history of the American people. In pondering this matter, therefore, I have often wondered if one could not discern a religious dimension even in the phototropic aspirations of a sunflower. In the life of a human being the complete absence of religious or spiritual concern is almost unimaginable.

With regard to self-conscious nations this religious dimension or some form of civil religion becomes an almost inevitable presence unless that nation has become so filled with injustice and resentment that its very existence as a nation is threatened. Even more basic than the civil religion of politically organized states, however, is

39

that almost universal and inescapable affection for a place which people in all ages have experienced and about which countless poems and sentimental songs have been written. It is often said that it is this nonpolitical love for a homeland that inspired the famous Roman testimony, *dulcet et decorum est pro patria mori*. All of us know these feelings and are quite right in regarding them as natural, humane and benign.

Because it is becoming an increasingly complex countercurrent in American life one should perhaps make a side comment on the ways in which immigrants to America from the seventeenth century to the present have continually modified their affection for this new land with a sad nostalgia for the old countries. In the process they, like native Americans, have sentimentalized those places to which they trace their roots. And for this primordial tendency of all non-nomadic people we all have a certain respect and sometimes even envy.

Yet there are also malignant forms of this same tendency which have arisen in modern times—most notably since the breakdown of Catholic universalism in the sixteenth century. The emergence of national self-consciousness, in fact, seems to have been one of the forces that led to the widespread dissatisfactions that precipitated the Protestant Reformation and then in turn led to the emergence of politically defined postfeudal states with a strong sense of having a religious mission. From this time forward national or political identity was often associated with a specific doctrinal position. Ulrich Zwingli is perhaps the first major reformer to die on the field of battle in a confessional cause—but there would be many others during the age of religious wars that followed.

In due time, moreover, what we may call modern nationalism came into existence. The nineteenth century was its great flowering time in the West. In the twentieth century it became a worldwide phenomenon. In his book, *The South and Sectional Conflict*, David M. Potter described the rise of nationalism "as the major political development of modern times." He also saw this new kind of patriotic passion as "one of the faiths that have replaced the religions of an earlier age."

For the vast majority of peoples whose fate it is to participate in the life of sovereign nations, there is still another fundamental human response which we must recognize and respect. I refer in the first place to the ways in which a clear sense of nationhood provides people with a needed sense of personal identity, a way of saying who one is. Edward Everett Hale once expounded this idea with a story about "The Man Without a Country," which used to be compulsory reading in the public schools. More recently, black Americans have addressed the same problem in an analogous but more militant mood.

Yet there is still another more clearly religious response that all citizens or subjects have felt, namely, an awareness of the state as an indubitably transcendent reality, an entity that exists above and beyond one's finite personhood, a collective form of human being in which one quite literally lives and moves and has one's being, but whose tendencies and actions one cannot individually change or steer—and to which, regardless of political circumstances, one is indeed "subject." This is an aspect of the human condition that Josiah Royce, and before him Hegel, did so much to illuminate— and to sublimate. Yet it is also a fact with which nearly all people must cope; it is thus a major source of that civil religion of which Rousseau spoke. Indeed, one might say that civil religion becomes inevitable and inescapable. The state becomes a transcendent source of moral norms; it often summons people to the ultimate sacrifice— often in an unjust cause.

I have a friend in Germany whose pastoral formation owed much to the writings of Bonhoeffer and Barth, and who was so alienated from the cold war stance of the postwar Adenauer government that he linked himself with Christian opposition movements. Yet when as a pastor he came to his first parish, he found that one of his first pastoral acts was expected to be the dedication of a stained-glass window in memory of the war dead. Pondering the fate of those boys who had been nurtured in the Hitler Jugend and had then been marched off to die in Russia or North Africa in response to the orders of a diabolical government, he decided that they deserved remembrance even more than the ordinary war dead. Their lives were *truly* tragic. And their parents' grief was often doubly deep.

In a similar manner, I think, we must see some virtue in those who are willing to serve in a war that they consider unjust—such as our late war in Southeast Asia. I know twin brothers who took opposite courses when their draft summonses came: one declared himself a conscientious objector, the other with the same negative view of the war could see no reason for exempting himself from a fate which so many youths of his generation unquestioningly accepted.

What one sees in these various considerations are some of the peculiar features of sovereign nations, or nation-states, or what Carlton J. H. Hayes and many others have seen as nationalistic religion. Most important is the fact that the simple existence of sovereign nations inescapably creates profound religious dilemmas. If one is the citizen of such a state, as we all are, one's fate or destiny is so caught up in the dynamics of nationhood that the religious dimensions of national aspiration are constantly manifest. Even if one accepts the essentially pessimistic eschatological doctrines of Dwight Lyman Moody—that this world (and hence surely this country with it) is a wrecked vessel and that only a lifeboat ride to the Parousia is available—the existential fact remains that each citizen is wedded to this or that nation until death parts him from it. We have no recourse but to resign ourselves to the fact that the state *is* a superhuman source of moral norms and to do our utmost to make them humane and just. It is in this context, moreover, that we must consider the rise and decline of that extraordinary form of civil religion or national faith which has shaped the destiny of the United States.

An undergraduate reporter for a college newspaper recently asked me what I meant by saying (as I do in my *A Religious History of the American People*) that "the moral and spiritual development of the American people is one of the most intensely relevant subjects on the face of the earth." The answer I gave was that if someone in Laos wondered why American airplanes year after year dropped more bombs on their little defenseless country than all the bombs we unloaded during the entire course of World War II (aside from the two very special bombs we reserved for Japan) that one of the best things such a person could do would be to study our "moral and religious history." I think that it would probably reveal more than a reading of general histories of our diplomacy or the histories of our economic and social and political development. From those forms of history the deepest kinds of animation and intentionality would be missing—as would our "aspirations." This is not to say that I see peoples and nations swept along in an inexorably flowing current: contingency and accident, even the unpredictable antics of climate and weather make changes—as they did during the "dust bowl years" of the New Deal or more massively and mysteriously in vast but slow social changes in Europe that projected fifty million Europeans into the greatest folk migration in world history. But nations do become the bearers of popular aspiration precisely because each person in them is for all practical purposes incapable of changing the course of human events and is committed to a given place and given government, and a given social order. The state thus becomes a transcendent factor in each citizen's life. The state determines the object of popular devotion. Anniversaries are solemnly observed in the national family as immemorially in the domestic family. Heroes and saints are remembered as well as historic moments and decisive events. Gratitude for those who sacrificed and suffered is expressed. Calls to emulation and loyalty are voiced. The cumulative effect of these activities, moreover, is a kind of collective consciousness, which in Royce's thought is seen as a genuine realm of the supernatural. To this realm Abraham Lincoln reverted or appealed in those desperate days of his First Inaugural address: "We are not enemies but friends. We must not be enemies. Though passion may have strained, it must not break, our bonds of affection. The mystic chords of memory, stretching from every battle-field and patriot grave to every living heart and hearthstone all over this broad land will yet swell the chorus of the Union when again touched, as surely they will be, by the better angels of our nature." In this light we do well to consider what Richard Niebuhr referred to as the "inner history" of our confession as Americans; and this I am convinced will have to carry us back far deeper into our past than the period our present bicentennary suggests.

The history of nationalism, of course, cannot be elaborated here but it is at least worth noting that the biblical picture of ancient Israel has always had a kind of prototypical influence in both the Christian and Moslem worlds and that the Protestant Reformation gave new force to the idea of a people's being chosen for a special mission in the world. Some have associated Oliver Cromwell and Puritanism with this impulse; others have seen the French Revolution as the birthplace of modern nationalism. As I have argued elsewhere, however, it is in America that the idea of religiopolitical nationalism was first fully institutionalized and culturally accepted. Indeed, we must go on to recognize that this "first new nation" declared its exceptional place in God's plan for this world in almost ultimate terms. It even located itself in the biblical narrative and felt no compunction about referring to itself as God's New Israel. The United States of America, in other words, became a datum of Christian theology. Given these facts and conditions the religious dimensions of this country's sense of mission are very easily discerned: they become identified with the nation's essential being, even though from very early times there have been many inhabitants of its "holy ground" who resented these extravagant claims and were bruised or oppressed by their practical implications.

In retelling this old, old story of America, therefore, one must be humble and circumspect. The present is a product of the whole past. There is not an event that does not leave its ineffaceable legacy. This whole finite world of ours stands between the Alpha and the Omega. As for the American Revolution which looms so large in our short history, its full significance could not be known without a God's-eye view of not only the whole past but the whole future as well. On the question of enduring significance historians must show very great restraint. Nevertheless, I do propose that there is an episode which we can fruitfully consider, and it has to do with the ways in which the Puritan impulse which arose in England and reached full expression in America became—through Providence, they would have said—the vanguard of the libertarian revolution in Western society.

G. K. Chesterton said it, and it has become one of the most widely quoted statements about America: "The United States is a nation with the soul of a church." Less widely quoted is his location of the basis for this assertion. It is not the commonly observed religiosity of the American people or the statistical fact that the country has a larger and more active church membership than any Western country. It is based on the alleged fact that "America is the only nation in the world that is founded on a creed." That creed, he went on to say, "is set forth with dogmatic, even theological, lucidity in the Declaration of Independence." Chesterton's analysis of this famous document is deficient and he had small interest in the historical background of the provincial Americans who had arrived at these libertarian conclusions, but he does at least pose an important question.

Jefferson went farther in his Second Inaugural address when he spoke of "that Being in whose hands we are, who led our forefathers, as Israel of old, from their native land and planted them in a country flowing with all the necessaries and comforts of life, who has covered our infancy with His providence and our riper years with His wisdom and power." John Adams, whose historical instincts ran deeper, was even more specific. What these men and the whole revolutionary generation knew was that the liberties Americans were even then enjoying were the results of a long struggle. Jonathan Mayhew had celebrated the centennial of Parliament's ultimate deed—the execution of Charles I in 1649—and the years from 1764 to 1776 had been filled with other reminders of that earlier revolution in England which Puritanism had inspired. It was this great struggle, said John Adams in 1765, "that peopled America, and after their arrival here these exiles began their settlement and formed their plan, both of ecclesiastical and civil government, in opposition to the canon and the feudal systems."

What we must see, therefore, is that the American Revolution will remain to us a conundrum and a mystery if we do not take into account that "revolution in Christendom" which was perpetrated by those English critics of traditional Christianity who began to shape a new notion of the church even in the days of Henry VIII and Edward VI, who became more determined in their designs while in exile in Bloody Mary's day, and who emerged as a powerful element in English society during the reign of Elizabeth. Animating this and succeeding generations of English church reformers were the deeds and sacrifices of the martyrs which had been rendered imperishable by John Foxe's great *Acts and Monuments,* his book of martyrs. In the spirit thus engendered, the reformers beheld England as an Elect Nation; England's duty, they insisted, was the defense of Protestants from the mignons of the antichrist in a wartorn world.

The idea of Elect Nationhood ineluctably carries us back to the word of God that Moses transmitted to Abraham's seed in the wilderness: "You are a Kingdom of priests, a holy nation." It was the prophetic force of monotheistic Judaism that would transform the Western world, though it would be mediated by the Christian church, which would identify itself as the New Israel, notably in the First Epistle of Peter: "Ye also as lively stones are built up a spiritual house, an holy priesthood. . . . ye are a chosen generation, a royal priesthood, an holy nation." By the year 311 A.D. Christianity became so great a power in the ancient world that the emperor himself had to capitulate if he wished to rule. And therewith did the chief elements of Hebraic religion become constitutive of Western civilization, above all conveying to it a radical sense of monotheistic orthodoxy and a conception of earthly reality as a linear historical movement from Creation to Consummation, from bondage to messianic fulfillment.

During the Middle Ages, to be sure, much of the church's prophetic force was lost due to the syncretic, otherworldly and universalistic tendencies of medieval Catholicism. The Reformation, however, was in its strictest sense a repudiation of the medieval church and its basic sense of religion. The Reformation was a biblical revival. It was also a time of emergent national feeling, with the result that many political entities began to be imbued with a sense of holy peoplehood, and this was especially true of those states which committed themselves to the reformed tradition in which, by 1536, John Calvin's great formulations of evangelical truth were being felt. Fundamental to this new teaching was a thoroughgoing repudiation of nearly every tangible aspect of the instituted Catholic Church and also an austere insistence on the absolute sovereignty of God, not only in history but in the saving of sinful man.

Nowhere did this course of events ensue with larger consequences (especially for America) than in England. Just why this should have been the case is not easily said; but at least two factors seem particularly relevant. First, the singular development of the English constitution, above all the House of Commons and the "liberties" guaranteed by the judicial system. Second, the country's unusually protracted Reformation experience—a process that begins even before Henry VIII made himself supreme head of England's Church (1530) and does not reach a stable settlement until 160 years of turmoil and violence were finally concluded by the Glorious Revolution of 1689.

England's Reformation entered an especially critical phase in 1558 when the death of Queen Mary brought the Protestant Elizabeth to the throne, and thus raised the great question as to what kind of Protestantism England would have. And in this situation a Puritan movement began to take shape. During the early years the major problems had to do with externals of church order: vestments, ceremonies, and practices which were associated with popery. More drastic by far was the unsuccessful effort to displace episcopacy altogether. During the later years of Elizabeth's reign, however, Puritan attention shifted to problems of salvation, election and hence to questions as to the marks of a true Christian and also of a truly Christian church.

In this latter context the teaching of William Perkins at Cambridge became especially important because of his powerful emphasis on the claim that the only real ground for assurance of election was the inward experience of God's regenerating grace. This may seem to be an innocuous doctrine but it was in fact a challenge to the almost universal practice of Christendom since the early Middle Ages. Not only did it introduce the subjective principle in matters of religion but it also raised doubts about the practice of the newer Protestant churches, including England's. In the long run its impact on church life and personal piety would be revolutionary. Some would say that it was a force that would make civil war inevitable.

Under King James I tensions increased and under King Charles I and Archbishop William Laud these tensions finally did erupt in civil war. The march of events in this Puritan revolution cannot be recounted here. But its deeds were drastic and Karl Marx was certainly correct in seeing it as the first real social revolution in the West. The Earl of Strafford, the Archbishop and the King were executed. Episcopacy, the House of Lords, and finally monarchy were abrogated. Religious liberty was declared and a new franchise instituted. And through it all one beholds the awesome figure of Oliver Cromwell, who, as Antonia Frazer suggests, might well be deemed the greatest of Englishmen.

As even American schoolchildren know, moreover, the spirit of this double Puritan revolution—religious and social—had fled to the American strand. Long before Cromwell's great victories America was becoming a "land of the Pilgrim's pride."

With a powerful sense of a providential destiny in the new world, colony after colony was founded, from Jamestown in 1607 to William Penn's Holy Experiment in Pennsylvania at the century's end, with all of them in varying ways populated by people who overwhelmingly shared the convictions and prejudices of Puritanism. In 1649 some of them, in the battle of the Severn, overran Lord Baltimore's Catholic proprietary in Maryland. During the Glorious Revolution they provoked disturbances—some of them violent—in every colony. During the wars of empire against the Spanish and French they discovered new dimensions of intercolonial solidarity. Out of the Great Awakenings came a rejuvenation of Puritan fervor and an increased sense of a millennial future for

America. Yet most momentous of all was the way that immi-
gration and intercolonial migration was steadily filling the land with
an individualistic and freedom-loving people who were practicing
their liberties in the ecclesiastical, social, economic and political
realms. It was a society such as the world had never seen.

Finally, after the great treaty of 1763 transferred all of New
France and the Floridas to British Protestant rule this people stood
prepared to enter what is referred to as the Revolutionary Epoch.
When that epoch ended—let us say in 1789 with the inauguration
of George Washington as the first president of a new federal republic—it could truly be said that liberties long claimed and increasingly wrought out in practice, in England first and then more
enduringly in America, had gained the formal constitutional guaran-
tees that had been so long desired. A revolution begun in 1640 had
reached its consummation.

Yet what had happened during the momentous period between
1775 and 1789 was not in the profound sense of the term a revolution—that had long since been carried out. Bernard Bailyn states
the case accurately: "What was essentially involved . . . was not
the disruption of American society . . . but the realization, comprehension, and fufillment of the inheritance of liberty, and of what
was taken to be America's destiny in the context of world history."
For this very reason, however, American exultation and extrava-
gance of statement knew no bounds. Even before the war had been
won, Timothy Dwight composed an anthem that made the ultimate
claim:

> Columbia, Columbia, Columbia, to glory rise,
> The queen of the world, and child of the skies:
> Thy reign is the last, and the noblest of time.

In 1831 a young Andover seminarian, Francis Smith, struck a note
that won even greater favor with the American people: "My
country, 'Tis of thee. . . ." Lyman Beecher would confidently repeat
the prophecy of Jonathan Edwards that the Kingdom of God
would commence in America. As the nation stood on the brink of
civil war, Julia Ward Howe's "Battle Hymn of the Republic" provided a statement that surpassed all the others in its power and
eloquence. And even after the collapse of Reconstruction there were
those who continued to insist on the nation's supreme place in God's
plan for a better world. So the songs of glory were sung on down

through the years of World War I, when Woodrow Wilson described the republic as a redeemer nation.

By this time, however, a countertrend had become noticeable. Dwight L. Moody best marks the turning when he reminded his vast revival audiences that this world is a "wrecked vessel." Then in 1929 came the great crash and the depression, as if to confirm the gloomier prognosis. In the turmoil and conflict of the 1960's patriotism of the old sort became an abomination to many and a credibility problem for many others. Then amid the scandals of the 1970's the idea of America as God's New Israel began to be seen as an unfortunate form of national arrogance for all but a minority of chauvinistic reactionaries. Urban insolvency, the near bankruptcy of worthy causes and humane institutions, and above all the persistent inability of the world's most affluent nation even to face (much less to solve) its massive problems of poverty, hunger, racism, and alienation had brought the republic to the point of ideological crisis. The country seemed to have become the victim of its libertarianism. Concern for distributive justice languished. Thirty million Americans seemed to be living almost outside the social covenant. Rancor, suspicion, and resentment were rife. The traditional civil religion no longer resonated in the public consciousness.

The nation seems to be standing between the times with no song to sing. It is doubtful, moreover, that ideological reconstruction can ensue until our boundless faith in an ever-larger gross national product yields to the desire for structural reform. In the meantime, we may hope that a rising concern for justice will create a dialectical relationship of liberty and equality that could in turn give substantial content to the idea of a nation dedicated to the general welfare.

The Drama of Good and Evil in American Writing

Alfred Kazin

. . . whilst I believe that evil is to be hated and resisted and punished, at least forcibly hindered, yet offences must needs come, and out of them comes good as naturally and inevitably as the beautiful flower and the nourishing fruit out of the dark ground. I believe that the tendency of all thought is to Optimism.

R.W. Emerson, *Journal*

The State is a poor, good beast who means the best: it means friendly. A poor cow who does well by you,—do not grudge it its hay. . . . But if you go to hook me when I walk in the fields, then, poor cow, I will cut your throat.

R.W. Emerson, *Journal*

Still, one loves America above all things, for her youth, her greenness, her plasticity, innocence, good intentions, friends, everything.

Wm. James, *Letters*

America is a didactic country whose people always offer their personal experiences as helpful lesson to the rest, hoping to hearten them and do them good—an intensive sort of personal relations project. . . . With everyone sold on the good how does all the evil get done?

Saul Bellow, *Humboldt's Gift*

God created Americans much like other people. But in the beginning all was good. America, being entirely new (at least to the white race), was especially good. Somehow Americans, simply because they were here and no longer there, considered themselves good people. They regarded themselves as being virtuous in the group because it, if not everyone in it, represented a new start for the weary sin-laden human race. The first moral aspiration of the Puritans was to be Israel reconstituted, a kingdom that rested on a covenant with God, its capital the holy city on the hill.

51

The Puritans were Calvinists, and had a proper insistence on the sinfulness and even treacherousness of the human heart. But the sovereignty of God was so total that the inequality of men had to be in God's plan. As Perry Miller pointed out long ago, Puritanism owed more to English social stratification than it did to Calvin's Geneva. God never knew his own mind so well as when he made certain newly arrived Puritans the prophets and theocratic administrators of a new society on this rude shore, one entirely in line with the only necessary revelation of his will—the Bible. To which we can add, with our knowledge of all the successors to the Puritans who came here as communities of virtuous believers, that as religious sectarians, fleeing in the group from persecution, the Puritans were more proud of their exceptionalism than they were despairing of human nature in general. The theme of a community of believers was to distinguish all those later arrivals who, whether or not they had actually suffered as a community for being Catholics or Jews or Mennonites or Quakers, regarded themselves as victims of religious persecution. Once they arrived here they enjoyed a special sense of their historic virtuousness—and this made possible their disdain for other religious sects in America.

Partisan theology played a decisive role in creating, within the Puritans' feeling that the elect must come from among them, a sense of being, if not a new Adam, the old Adam in a new, fresh setting. In the beginning, said John Locke, all was America. The creation of man and the world in the Old Testament was somehow conflated with the newness of being on this continent. It was not that man was considered naturally good—though this extraordinary supposition was to flower in the nineteenth century under the benevolent eye of transcendentalism, and to inaugurate what we now think of as a distinctively native literature. But the continent being new and sparsely inhabited by savages, arrivals on this shore could think of their exertions and their suffering as a renewal of the spirit—a kind of baptism in the astoundingly redemptive medium that was the New World.

Moral aspiration was unbounded. As late as 1900, Henry James in England could say of *The Ambassadors* that "there are degrees of merit in subjects . . . . What it comes to is that even among the supremely good, since with such alone is it one's theory of one's honour to be concerned—there is an ideal *beauty* of goodness the invoked action of which is to raise the artistic faith to its maximum

. . . *The Ambassadors*, I confess, wore this glow for me from the beginning to the end. . . ."

Herman Melville, who was to hymn the "power of blackness" in our literature, nevertheless identified America with historic virtuousness. In *Redburn* (1849), the novelized account of his hard, bitter voyage to England as a cabin boy in 1839, he wrote: "I had learned to think much and bitterly before my time; all my young mounting dreams of glory had left me; and at that early age, I was as unambitious as a man of sixty." Yet arriving in England and overwhelmed by the indifference of the English to people starving, neglected, dying in the streets of Liverpool, the young Redburn becomes ecstatic about his own country as he watches the immigrant ships loading up for America:

> Our blood is as the flood of the Amazon, made up of a thousand noble currents all pouring into one. We are not a nation, so much as a world; for unless we may claim all the world for our sire, like Melchisedec, we are without father or mother.
>
> For who was our father and our mother? . . . Our ancestry is lost in the universal paternity; and Caesar and Alfred, St. Paul and Luther, and Homer and Shakespeare are as much ours as Washington. . . . We are the heirs of all time, and with all nations we divide our inheritance. On this Western Hemisphere all tribes and people are forming into one federated whole; and there is a future which shall see the estranged children of Adam restored as the old hearth-stone in Eden.
>
> The other world beyond this, which was longed for by the devout before Columbus' time, was found in the New; and the deep-sea lead, that first struck these soundings, brought up the soil of Earth's Paradise. Not a Paradise then, or now; but to be made so, at God's good pleasure, and in the fullness and mellowness of time. The seed is sown, and the harvest must come; and our children's children, on the world's jubilee morning, shall all go with their sickles to the reaping. Then shall the curse of Babel be revoked, a new Pentecost come, and the language they shall speak shall be the language of Britain. Frenchmen, and Danes, and Scots; and the dwellers on the shores of the Mediterranean, and in the regions round about; Italians, and Indians, and Moors; there shall appear unto them cloven tongues as of fire.

A rhapsody by a man of genius, not any more logical than the rhapsodies over America, or more precisely over the *idea* of America, made by many another lonely and embittered American in Europe. The exultancies are biblical, as they so often are in Melville. Behind them lie some Hebraic connotations of history as existing for *our* sake, the Bible as intimate to our deepest wishes, that made John Jay Chapman say that the "heart of the world is Jewish." Theologically, Hebrew thought believes that, ideally, man is not so much good as he is purposive. History, as it shows the hand of God in our lives, is thus his domain.

So the drama of history turned to working itself out here, in the newest of new "worlds." It was so new that all the earliest associations with it were of some special grace, so new that the liberation of European thought from the sixteenth century on was identified with the discovery of America. Tocqueville, no romantic and still the most judicious and profound analyst of democracy in America from a traditionalist, Catholic point of view, said that America was discovered as if it had been held in waiting by the deity. No wonder that in the comparative absence of lived history, the idea of history on this continent made Americans as a group seem virtuous to themselves. Some divine purpose was manifesting itself through them. You have only to think of the incorrigible optimism of the Jews despite their tortured history to realize what it means to believe that you have a covenant with the maker of this world. Puritanism, despite its programmatic suspicions of human nature as inherently and universally depraved, developed even more deeply, on American soil, an idea of a special relationship with God based on the Englishman's own energy, hope and cooperation against the heathen hostile Indian. If man's wickedness is demonstrated by his unhappiness and ingratitude, man's rapid progress and "conquest" of the New World could not help but give him a better opinion of himself. Anglo-Saxon race pride, a very considerable factor in the notable self-esteem of New Englanders, worked here as it did everywhere in imperialist history to show the superiority of the dominating power. And as the Calvinist apologists of slavery were to note with the same smugness, God evidently meant to put white over black.

Now if you multiply all this by the national pride that grew out of the Revolution, especially in the era of nationalistic expansion that developed after the second war with the mother country in 1812, you see how the groundwork of an *American* literature was laid in this distinct belief: the natural and *national* virtuousness of Americans. This amounted to folklore. A republic, *res publica*, founded by definition, by design, aimed at public happiness. The eighteenth-century political Calvinism of the Founders expressed itself in a sober belief in human improvement through politics; the natural excess of man was held in by checks and balances. Between the rationalism that expressed itself in the Declaration as optimism and the Calvinism that expressed itself in the moral superiority of American Revolutionary heroes, self-approval abounded. There had never been such a principled government.

So much political virtue did not mean innocence. It meant positive ideals, as in the Declaration, and rational safeguards, as in the Bill of Rights and the separation of powers. American virtuousness was meanwhile inseparable from rural frugality and independence, the optimism of a new and growing country with a seemingly unlimited frontier, and above all the Protestant sense that virtue was evidenced by material progress. Jay Gatsby, bootlegger and racketeer, had no less reason to doubt his essential virtuousness than did George F. Baer, Pierpont Morgan's legal adviser, a railroad and coal baron who in 1902 refused to arbitrate the strike of anthracite coal miners. "The rights of the laboring man will be protected and cared for, not by labor agitation, but by the Christian men to whom God in his infinite wisdom has given control of the property interests of this country." John D. Rockefeller said humbly: "God gave me my money." And the further west you went, the more it was God's own country. One big moral aspiration was always to enlist God on your side.

God was somehow not a divine person or supernatural force so much as he was a ritualistic name identified with peace, plenty, freedom, happiness. He was, even more than "Nature's God," as Jefferson put it in the Declaration, Nature itself—that is, the principle of growth and progress. America was man's second chance, "the world's best hope," that Jefferson saw behind American settlement and the American Revolution: America as Nature, Nature as Beneficence, Man as the crown of Nature. In rural isolation this became the peaceable kingdom in the iconography of so many Quakers, Mennonites, Shakers and other virtuous separatists. Despite the fiercely exclusive sectarianism of so many American creeds, there was significant if unadmitted agreement that God had been brought to earth, that God expressed himself in the sublimity of men. This was a short move, all in the American pattern, to the romantic pantheism of Emerson, Thoreau and Whitman that indeed God and nature were interchangeable terms.

Soon "man" was to be slipped into this equation, but only if he was a great poet or "prophet" of American possibility.

Inherently, God in America represented himself, if he could not always personify himself, as a paradise on earth. Man even to Jefferson was not perfectible, but he was certainly teachable insofar as he was open to reason as the necessary persuader of one's best interests. The highest interest was the public happiness.

Now, on the brink of the American revolution in literature, which was performed by ex-ministers like Emerson and would-be or self-proclaimed saints like Thoreau and Whitman, the real and enduring American religion showed itself as a popular religion of optimism and easy sympathy. Even Jonathan Edwards had defined "true virtue as benevolence to being in general. Or perhaps to speak more accurately, it is that consent, propensity and union of the heart to being in general, which is immediately exercised in general good will. . . ." Calvinism among the intellectual elite at Harvard had long since been diffused into the ethical voluntarism of Unitarianism, the sympathy with all forms of being that Channing had set as the ground of emancipation from too-fixed creeds. Unitarianism was still too credal and rigid for Emerson. This first great American writer, significantly a founder of *modern* literature, turned his extraordinary gifts, as religious as they were literary, into such a fusion of orphic religion and esthetic subtlety that to this day it has proved impossible to separate Emerson the visionary from Emerson the cunning stylist.

Emerson's aspiration was "simple," astounding; every American, in the fullness of his private imagination, could be, like Emerson, poet, prophet, man of genius with universal interest. Emerson preached, he exhorted, but he did this by intoxicating. "Trust thyself: all hearts vibrate to that iron string." "The kingdom of man over nature, which cometh not with observation—a dominion such as now is beyond his dream of God—he shall enter without more wonder than the blind man feels who is gradually restored to perfect sight." "Let me admonish you, first of all, to go alone; to refuse the good models, even those which are sacred in the imagination of men, and dare to love God without mediator or veil. . . . Yourself a new born bard of the Holy Ghost, cast behind you all conformity, and acquaint men at first hand with Deity. Look to it first and only, that fashion, custom, authority, pleasure, and money, are nothing to you—are not bandages over your eyes, that you cannot see—but live with the privilege of the immeasurable mind."

If the supreme type of the European writer is Shakespeare, because he is all dialectic, plays on language, human interchange and dramatic conflict, Emerson more than any other incarnates the moral aspiration of the American writer toward a religion of goodness, harmony, perfect equanimity between man and man, man and nature, man and God. This was a wish for sameness. The lack of differentiation in Emerson's ideal America is typical of a purely religious morality. Emerson preached the individual self as immeasurable mind. What this meant was that all men must seek the same goals as propounded by a wholly visionary private religion. Transcendentalism as opposed to mere literature (the kind we unregenerate moderns have) betrays its religious bias by emphasizing Man, not men. And Man to Emerson meant a man of letters living comfortably in a pleasant New England town like Concord whose only physical exertions were walking and talking with men as benign as himself.

Henry James in *The American Scene* wrote condescendingly of Concord that it was a charming "woodsy, watery place, for so long socially and typically and above all interestingly homogeneous." He added that "this left the effect of something ineffaceable." And indeed Emerson's genius and his influence are the same. In the age of Norman Mailer the American writer carries on the myth of being a self-starter. No good writer with us ever admits that he takes off from tradition as Europeans do. But what James also emphasized about "watery and woodsy" Concord was that Emerson's goodness was kept inviolate by his provincialism. Concord was certainly a peaceable kingdom—it still lacks a movie house. But even John Jay Chapman, who understood Emerson's amazing abilities as a writer, admitted that you can learn more about life from an Italian opera than you can from the works of Ralph Waldo Emerson, for at least in Italian opera there are two sexes.

This is not the place to discuss more fully the ostentatious sexual purity of transcendentalism, for it is much richer in Puritan race pride than it is in manly sacrifice. Everything touching on sex is strange and secret in Thoreau, too romantic to be understood just now. Thoreau's moral aspiration was for a perfect attachment with nature. "I enter on my woodland walk as the homesick go home." Thoreau is comic in his priggishness, tragic in his sublimated passion for bushes, berries and Walden Pond even in

winter. But when Thoreau complained of *Leaves of Grass* that it
was as if "the beasts spoke," his tension as a man and writer
betrayed him into the typically Puritan—because biblical—belief
that good and evil exist mostly as sexual entities. When John Brown
was hanged, Thoreau was to awaken to a no less subjective idea of
evil. Magnificently deluded as he was about John Brown as the
avenging archangel (of death) rooting out slavery, Thoreau knew
as little about slavery as he did about sex. He judged both from
lofty abstractions that satisfied his sense of New England's moral
superiority. But if there had not been so much chilling virtuousness
in the air, there mightn't have been such powerful images of corruption in Poe, so much dynamic and even apocalyptic awareness
of human illusion and domination in Melville, so much awareness
of the treacheries of human nature and even the *economics* of passion in Henry James, so much celebration of homoerotic love in
Whitman, so much contempt even in Dickinson for the profession-
ally good ladies of "good society."

Our greatest nineteenth-century writers are sexual eccentrics,
sexual heretics. There seems to be some relation between that and
the fact that these same writers—Thoreau, Melville, Whitman,
Dickinson—were ignored or banned or despised in their own time.
When Americans still thought of purity as indigenous American
virtue, the unconscious rebellion of the creative spirit was not
against control—it was against moral coerciveness in all fields. It
was against sameness as a form of morality. Literature, as we can
see in Whitman's pretensions to the roles of Osiris and Christ, had
no recognized autonomy until after the Civil War. In some way,
then, Poe's imagination took the form of what his admirer
Baudelaire was to call "flowers of evil." Poe was the first major
intelligence we had in American literature to direct himself entirely
toward esthetic questions. His *conscious* intelligence was formidable
and, alas, he knew this all too well. One can say that Poe's greatest
aspiration was personally to be a Magus of literature, a prophet
and magician from the sacred precincts of poetry to an audience of
disciples. But Poe's *unconscious* intelligence was morbid, sickly,
self-pitying. The perfect subject for a poem, he declared, was the
death of a beautiful woman. He was a prisoner of sex always in
psychic extremes—so he wrote the most extreme allegories of the
artist's isolation in the New World out of his fantasies of destruc-
tiveness and necrophilia.

Politically, Poe was a haughtily reactionary apologist for slavery. Like Carlyle, D. H. Lawrence and other sexually crippled geniuses, he had fantasies of a master race and of himself leading it. And not unlike the Southern "fugitive" poets who became famous in the early twentieth century by opposing themselves to modern industrial and urban society, Poe was didactic by nature to an audience he affected to despise. But his unconscious sense of sex was not just morbid but hallucinatory. As with Melville, Thoreau, Dickinson, even Emerson in his great essay on "The Poet," the *mythological* manifestation of sex was the real vitality of these writers. Thoreau is never so spontaneous as when he is talking about the harshness of Mount Katahdin in Maine—one of the few real outbreaks in his writing. "What is this Titan that has possession of me? Talk of mysteries! Think of our life in nature—daily to be shown matter, to come in contact with it . . . *Contact! Contact! Who* are we? *where* are we?" Melville on the sea, apart from his homoerotic addiction to many heroes—Jack Chase in *White Jacket,* Bulkington and even Ahab in *Moby-Dick,* Captain Vere in *Billy Budd*—had the most intense gift for mythologizing human desire. Under the pursed mouth of official American morality, tremendous currents of passionate imagination were breaking out. The artist discovers himself not in generalizing doctrine, but in the association of his secret life with great nature itself.

Melville, as his baffled and disdainful contemporaries recognized without knowing that they did, was a rebel against God, a blasphemer by nature who proved his obsession by railing against it. "I have written a wicked book," he wrote to Hawthorne after *Moby-Dick,* "and feel as spotless as the lamb." "I baptize thee," shrieks crazy Ahab in "The Forge" chapter, "not in the name of the Father, but in the name of the Devil!" Melville's aspiration was entirely toward the heroic. He saw his prime characters as contenders with the sea, fate, other men—and as in the case of magnificent murdering Ahab, one's own insatiable will. So we get a picture of man in a universe distinctly meant for man to be at home in, a universe that allows man every magnificent challenge, but always has the last word.

Emerson said that nature was "meant to serve." Evil, he said, is just "privative"—it takes away. In short, the universe—world: nature: God—terms indistinctly the same to these American romantics, meaning all that is not myself—is still man-centered. But here is Ishmael-Melville on the whiteness of the whale, a passage which the infinite silence of our ever more alien world has made far more significant to us than to the churchly missionary papers that condemned *Moby-Dick* in 1851.

> Though in many of its aspects this visible world seems formed in love, the invisible spheres were formed in fright. . . .
> Is it that by its indefiniteness it shadows forth the heartless voids and immensities of the universe, and thus stabs us from behind with the thought of annihilation, when beholding the white depths of the milky way? . . . as an essence whiteness is not so much a color as the visible absence of color . . . is it for these reasons that there is such a dumb blankness, full of meaning, in a wide landscape of snows—a colorless, all-color of atheism from which we shrink?

Melville is talking about a world beyond deciphering, except in terms of force, and perhaps about the insufficiency or final narcissism of what Whitman called manly love. Whitman turned his longings into a political myth of comradeship with the wounded soldiers he was tending in Washington hospitals, the martyred Lincoln figuring as the great western fallen star. Whitman's greatest aspiration was toward unity in every sense, but always on his own terms—unity between the present and the future, as in *Crossing Brooklyn Ferry*, between the One and the Many, between nature and spirit, between the poet and the masses. It is ironic to think that Whitman's marginal sexuality should have flowered into so many stereotyped images of America.

But the point to be made about this is that the triumph of capitalism in the Civil War and the emergence of America as the greatest material power in history made secondary all these personal sexual myths. The aspiration of the new realistic writers—James, Mark Twain, Crane, Dreiser, even Dickinson—was toward the truth of the necessarily enigmatic relationships between men and emphatically between man and woman now, in a godless universe. Man becomes entirely a civic character, a symbol, at most, of his society. Behind the so-called infinitude of the private mind, as Emerson had blissfully preached it, had lain the fact that God, taken out of the heavens and reduced to a hazardous life on earth as the power of nature, or man's "wish" for access to the divine energy, turned the self into an *instrument* for self-advancement.

Under the reign of what William James was to call the "bitch-goddess," or the dream of success, was to emerge openly (it was always implicit in the myth of America as a new start for humanity) the theme of human striving as too often an ego system.

The myth of the universe as Nature, or infinite power, now shows itself in Mark Twain, Stephen Crane, Dreiser, Robinson, Frost, the young Eliot, as a world colder than the polar world of Gordon Pym and Captain Ahab. What disappears after the Civil War is the metaphysical hero, the conscious intellectual bravado, that had tried to live with theology in the absence of religion. America is hardly a "divine" experiment to the Mark Twain who said bitterly: "it was wonderful to discover America, it would have been more wonderful to lose it." The ethical, in Henry James's praise of "goodness" as the ideal subject for the novelist, supplants the visionary. But of course: "things are in the saddle, and ride mankind." The myth of some ideal freedom for the individual, the artist's favorite image, leads under the most ruthless industrial and commercial organization, to a split between the men of affairs, whether in politics or in the corporation establishment, and a rag-tail and bobtail mob of writers, dissidents, immigrant "anarchists" bringing up the rear with futile complaints.

The politicoes before World War II understood nothing of the world outside America. How different they were from the managers of America's superpower since 1945, who are plainly more involved in every international question than in the humdrum injustices of American society. McKinley knew so little, or deceived himself so much, that he said we went to war with Spain to "Christianize" the Philippines. Wilson at Versailles was heard by Felix Frankfurter to say: "If I didn't feel that I was the personal instrument of God, I couldn't carry on." The public men, as we know from the godly example of Richard Nixon, were to carry on like advertising men who come to believe their own concoctions—at least in public.

But the writers, more and more private men in every sense, now demonstrate their thorough skepticism about America's official and public philosophy—which is now salesmanship of whatever our public men *think* they believe at the moment they deliver their ghost-written commercials. Even to successful men of letters like Mark Twain, William Dean Howells, Henry James, our vaunted constitutional freedom did not represent economic justice, racial tolerance or peaceful national purpose. James in his richest novel about the rich, *The Golden Bowl,* a truly resplendent performance, unerringly had his billionaire protagonist say: "We're tremendously moral for ourselves—that is, for each other." He spoke of a "corrupt and falsified and demoralized generation."

Hawthorne, the least radical and polemical of writers, had doubted the morality of American business and had profoundly distrusted the North's motives in the Civil War. But the alienation of Hawthorne, Poe, and Melville from the American majority that equated democracy with the best of all possible worlds and American Protestantism with exclusive wisdom, was as nothing compared with the divergence of the best writers from America's public optimism, public egalitarianism, public sanctity. The heart of the matter is the difference between religion as a form of rhetoric and national salesmanship—one nation under God, the family that prays together stays together, Nixon's prayer breakfasts—and the increasing complexity and conflict within the writer's mind as he saw that America was obviously more secularized than it professed or knew or cared.

America even before the era of modern power had been more concerned with theology than with faith. The American hope even more than the American experience was concerned with a God who is altogether of this world. In older countries religion was a cultural and even a national tradition because the supernatural and the transcendent, as Plato first recognized, is in the very nature of human thought. Sainte-Beuve was to say of the French that they remained Catholics even when they had ceased to be Christians. With us there was no general agreement on theology—far from it!—and yet everything in the American way of making progress on this continent conspired against a committed supernaturalism. The churches were bent, each in its own way, on salvation; but salvation was so intimately tied up with success that it is safe to say that failure was an admission of guilt. There is no way of being honorably poor in America. If this seems not to be as true of the youth of the recent past, it is because the children of the middle class could play at poverty as the children of the poor could not, and because the boom-and-bust pattern of our economy had disillusioned the young—who, incidentally, play at social change as if they were playing at art. "Art" has indeed become a form of mass hedonism.

Among writers after the Civil War who came from families with a strong interest in religion—Dickinson, Clemens, James, Crane, Dreiser—there was a noticeable reaction against orthodoxy. The real American tradition for such writers was the Emersonian belief that only the unchurched individual has access to divine revelation. But their moral aspiration was not to a universe synonymous with moral order but to the truth of a human experience that constantly eludes every attempt to generalize it. Emerson once dreamed that the universe was an apple revolving in space and that he ate it—at one bite. Emily Dickinson even as an adolescent at orthodox Mount Holyoke refused to term herself a believer. The truth, say her poems—the most flawless body of major poetry written by an American in her century—is that the individual is metaphysically unsheltered. Her favorite theme is *how we die*— and we are surrounded by those who think that their fears and professions of faith give them some knowledge of an experience of which even we, as we die, cannot communicate until it is too late. She avows, with the greatest philosophic humor in all American literature, not that there is another realm, but that we may be on the brink of it. Certainty is beyond our knowledge and power.

> I know that He exists.
> Somewhere—in Silence—
> He has hid his rare life
> From our gross eyes.
>
> 'Tis an instant's play.
> 'Tis a fond Ambush—
> Just to make Bliss
> Earn her own surprise!
>
> But—should the play
> Prove piercing earnest—
> Should the glee—glaze—
> In Death's—stiff—stare—
>
> Would not the fun
> Look too expensive!
> Would not the jest—
> Have crawled too far!

Evil, it now seemed, was not the deprivation of good, as Emerson had thought, but the *nullity*, the positive *insignificance* of

man in a universe definitely not constructed to his personal satisfaction. Stephen Crane, son of a famous Methodist clergyman, wrote
that Art is the child of Pain and that an artist "is nothing but a
powerful memory that can move itself at will through certain experiences sideways and every artist must be in some things powerless
as a dead snake." In one of his most frightening images of our old
moral world out of orbit, he described Nebraska in winter. "One
viewed the existence of man then as a marvel, and conceded a
glamour of wonder to these lives which were caused to cling to a
whirling, fire-smitten, ice-locked, disease-stricken, space-lost bulb."

Yet beyond all outrage to our insignificance as individuals lay
the overriding triumph of American power. This had been going
on, abroad as well as at home, said Henry Adams, from the
beginnings of the republic. The real theme on everybody's mind
was how to make it, the real desire of every true American was
to succeed as his country had succeeded. The central image America provided to its own people was the trend upwards: *The Rise of
American Civilization, The Rise of Silas Lapham, Up from Slavery,
The Americanization of Edward Bok,* even *The Rise of David
Levinsky.* The Business of America Is Business, said Calvin
Coolidge—to which all the new social satirists in effect replied: the
business of American writers is to show up people like Calvin
Coolidge.

Evil to American writers in the first half of the twentieth
century was the Jungle, the stockyards, child labor, the House of
Morgan in 1917 dragging us into war to protect its swinish invest-
ments. Evil was nothing but the excesses of the profit system. To
judge by what he said, the American novelist from *The Jungle* to
The Grapes of Wrath had only one aspiration: a fair shake and a
new deal for the oppressed and forgotten. But only when World
War II ended the depression and the U. S. emerged from it in 1945
stronger and with the conviction that it possessed unlimited power
over nature as well as over its only possible rival superpower, some
ancient warnings about the nature and meaning of seemingly unlimited power came to writers' minds.

"A people that has the power to destroy all life on this planet,"
said Francois Mauriac, "should not have a vulgar laugh." It was a
time when the unbridled sense of power bred typical rich man's
talk about an "American century." A paranoiacally suspicious
nationalism that made a proto-Marxist ideology out of America

itself fostered in the name of "loyalty" every kind of intimidation of "politically unreliable" individuals. Writers on the whole went their own way, which is why *Life* magazine, that cocktail in pictures, announced with righteous contempt that the American writer gave the appearance of a homosexual living in a garbage pail.

Yet even Henry Luce, the Presbyterian missionary's son, was mindful of the natural depravity of the human heart. Luce just saw no connection between the illusion of unlimited power and the crazy inflation of everything material, functional, mechanical. Luce's typical media image of U.S. life was unreal, just as his claim to an American century was stupid and therefore unreal. But now the poets and novelists and critics from the 1940's on recognized that the real theme was the growing unreality of all public and official images. Truth, sometimes hopelessly complex and as frightening as a scream in the night, was more like a specter of the increasing alienation between man and his increasing brutalization and poisoning of the earth. The domination over nature by "Nature's Nation" was mocking man through his own fears of radiation sickness, the spreading cancer menace, and annihilation more real than the author of *Moby-Dick* could have dreamed of.

The ego system was defeating the most innocent aspirations of man himself. "To the outermost spaces," Werner Heisenberg wrote, "man carries only the image of himself." Khrushchev duly noted that the Soviet astronauts had gone far, very far into the heavens without finding God. Soviet writers were silent. But in the frenzied, sometimes hallucinated, urban landscapes of the new American writers—Lowell, Mailer, Bellow, Plath, Heller, Pynchon —one saw and heard insistencies that pointed to unadmitted issues. The human will had turned rhetorical. As society felt increasingly threatened by its own runaway technology, the word itself seemed fragmentized and literature superfluous. Yet the writer knew that at least he was after reality, while the Nixons did not even know that they had abandoned it. Mailer before the Vehicle Assembly Building in the space center at Cape Kennedy, Heller on the madness that in the bureaucracy of the army is institutionalized as normalcy, Plath writing at daybreak in her London kitchen about her fear of the Nazi as a universal type, Lowell on the uprooting of the Boston common to make still another garage, Bellow in New York on the exhaust gas level in the air with our faces, Pynchon on the great bomb intended for the enemy that sooner or later hangs over our own head—these are the images of a world that really exists, that grows every day more disruptive, but which is known and accepted only in fragments, in concrete words, in the conjointed actions of writing, sentence by sentence.

The most astonishing thing about evil, as always, is that it sits side by side with us, with everything ordinary, yet claims not to exist. But the voice of the good, which I reluctantly equate with the honesty and perseverance of the intelligence in all desperate cases like our own, is, as Freud said, "soft but persistent."

What wild hopes our writers still hold out to us. The hope lies in their ability to present, to render for us as no one else does, the imagination of power which we conceived as residing entirely on our side, but which, as in some mysterious fable warning against man the overreacher, plots against us. We placed all our hopes in our sovereignty over what Emerson called "Nature"—what is not ourselves—and find that in its recoil this supposed object of our power uses us even more than we use it. I think of Mailer in *Of a Fire on the Moon,* standing in the largest possible room, the Vehicle Assembly Building at Cape Kennedy—

> but he was standing at least in the first cathedral of the age of technology and he might as well recognize that the world would change, that the world *had* changed. . . . And it had changed in ways he did not recognize, had never anticipated, and could possibly not comprehend now. The change was mightier than he had counted on. The full brawn of the rocket came over him in this cavernous womb of an immensity, this giant cathedral of a machine designed to put together another machine which would voyage through space. Yes, this emergence of a ship to travel the ether was no event he could measure by any philosophy he had been able to put together in his brain.

How far we have gone in little more than a century of American writing from Emerson's "Nature is meant to serve" to our recognition that, as always, we serve *it,* are part of its process. But nature does not ask questions. We do. Nature is not concerned with good and evil, not even with any discrimination between them. We are. That is what literature is about. Our own lives are at stake.

Science and the Growth
of the American Republic

I. Bernard Cohen

Just a few years ago, it was estimated that 90 percent of all the scientists and engineers who had ever lived were still alive; and that more than half of them were resident in the United States. These numbers show the status of America as a major scientific nation,* and the reason why this is a fact of critical importance for the historical analyst in 1976 is that only 40 years ago America could probably still be classed as an "undeveloped" (or "developing") country on the highest scale of the international scientific community. Before addressing myself to the causes of this change and its consequences for American political and social thought and action, for the American conscience and for America's public image and self-image, let me indicate the kind of evidence that supports my assertion that America might be considered "underdeveloped" with respect to the sciences, prior to 1935. First of all, there was an almost wholly one-way direction of movement of graduate and post-doctoral students:† eastward over the Atlantic to the great Euro-

---

* This statement, that 90 percent of all the scientists who have ever lived are still alive, is usually attributed to Professor Edward Purcell of Harvard, but he stoutly denies ever having made it. It was given wide currency, coupled with the name of Purcell, by J. Robert Oppenheimer, in an article entitled, "The Tree of Knowledge," published in *Harper's* magazine in October, 1958. The added remark that of these scientists and engineers "nearly half of them live in the United States," occurs on page 27 of the volume devoted to the United States, in the series "Reviews of National Science Policy," published by the Organization for Economic Cooperation and Development. The grounds for our being able to say that 80 or 90 percent of all the scientists who have ever lived are still living may be found in the opening pages of Derek J. DeSolla Price, *Little Science, Big Science.*

The estimate that half of these scientists and engineers are now residing in the United States must be something of an exaggeration. For instance, according to a report published in 1959 by OECD, the total number of scientists and engineers in the USA was somewhat greater than in all the other OECD countries taken together (that is, Austria, Belgium, Canada, France, Greece, Italy, Sweden, United Kingdom, Yugoslavia): 1,096,000 in the USA and 973,500 for the others. Since these figures do not include the Soviet Union, China, Japan, India, and other non-OECD countries, the "half" referred to is clearly wrong. Even so, the proportion of scientists and engineers in the United States to those of the other OECD countries cited above does at least validate the claim that by the early 1960's America had become one of the foremost nations in the world in science.

† It must be remembered, as a qualifier, that the movement of graduate

pean centers of scientific teaching and research. Although there were some fields in which Americans had been making outstanding contributions, such as experimental and theoretical genetics, by and large the great overarching theories that either introduced order into one of the sciences, or brought diverse branches of science into an unexpected relationship, or revolutionized much of science, were produced by Europeans: Rutherford, the Curies, Einstein, Bohr, Pauli, Heisenberg, Schrödinger, Dirac.* In 1963, in an address on the occasion of the centenary celebrations of our National Academy of Sciences, John F. Kennedy observed that of the 670 members of the Academy, 163 (or one out of every four) had been born in foreign lands—a figure that differed in order of magnitude from the condition in any other country, and that showed the degree to which the high estate that American science had gained was owing to the infusion of scientists from abroad.†

There can be no doubt whatsoever that by the 1960's America had become the pacesetter in science for the whole world. Our annual expenditures for scientific research and development were not only large in themselves but by the mid-1960's represented the world's peak of 3 percent of the GNP (gross national product), not even closely matched by most other advanced countries.‡ But

students and postdoctoral graduate students can never purely reflect the difference between the attractiveness of American centers of research and European ones, since there is always a factor of availability of funds to support such travel. An examination of the sources of support for Americans, for example, shows the good luck in having such funds made available through the Rockefeller Foundation (the Institute for International Education). Furthermore, there can be no doubt that there were some real attractions to Europeans in America, such as the existence of observatories with large telescopes.

* A somewhat different point of view might appear from an intensive study of the activity of Americans during the first three decades of the twentieth century, in agricultural, biomedical, and life sciences. For there can be no doubt that Americans were making more first-rate contributions in these areas than in the exact and physical sciences. Furthermore, there was no succession of overarching theories, of the sort exemplified by quantum theory or relativity or atomic structure, in these life and health sciences. Yet the general impression held by American and by European scientists is that America had not achieved an overall highest rank in these areas either, until the fourth decade of the twentieth century.

† Again, numbers by themselves do not provide conclusive evidence. For instance, it might have been the case that this large proportion of Europeans was due to the fact that America had become so great a scientific country that many European and Asian scientists had emigrated here — drawn to our great centers of research activity.

‡ The only country that came even reasonably close to an annual R&D budget of 3 percent of the GNP in these years was the United Kingdom. In the

there is some difference of opinion as to when it was that America actually became a first-rate scientific power. Some would date America's arrival to this highest estate only in the post-World War II era, others would see this occurring in the late thirties (with the advent of the European refugees and of those free-minded spirits who found America a more congenial home than the Europe of the dictators), while there are even others who (optimistically, in my opinion) see the emergence of America as a first-rate scientific power on a worldwide scale even earlier in the century. But there are none, to my knowledge, who would take a stand so outrageously contradictory to historical evidence as to assign America's advent to such scientific majority to the first or second decade of the twentieth century.

The change in America's scientific status has been accompanied by a tremendous shift in the sources of support for science. In the decade from 1930 to 1940, scientific research and development by industry accounted for approximately 70 percent of the total annual budget for American scientific research and development, with a bare 11 percent for university research and a mere 16 percent being spent by the federal government in all of its scientific activities. In these years, the total budget for research and development rose from $160 million in 1930 to $340 million in 1940. At this time the total annual R&D expenditures were at a modest level of 0.3 percent of the gross national product. By 1965-1967, when the annual R&D expenditures rose to 3 percent of the GNP, the total budget for those years was of the order of $20 billion. But, whereas in the thirties the federal government's share had been a mere 16 percent, in the mid-sixties this contribution had become a mammoth 64 percent. Of this latter sum, the giant's share was taken by a few mission-oriented agencies: the Department of Defense, the National Aeronautics and Space Administration, and the Atomic Energy Commission. Although the federal government finances this 64 percent of all R&D funds, it performs only 15 percent of the work in its own laboratories and institutions. To put it another way, only some 36 percent of the total R&D budget is nongovernmental in its source of financial support, which comes from industry, foundations, and universities; but 85 percent of all R&D is actually done in the private sector. As an aside, it may be noted that when it comes to

Soviet Union, however, matters are reckoned somewhat differently, and it has been estimated that the equivalent would now be at least 3 percent of the GNP.

basic science or fundamental research, the government still supplies
about 64 percent of the funds, but the work is carried out overwhelmingly in universities.* Two final statistics: in 1974 the annual
expenditure of the Department of Agriculture for basic research
alone was of the same order of magnitude as the total annual budget
of the United States in 1930 for fundamental and applied research
and development; and in that same year 1974, the basic research
expenditures through the National Science Foundation by far ex-
ceeded the total budget for research and development of the United
States in 1940 (which was more than twice what it had been in
1930).

It is difficult to tell exactly when each of the separate branches
of science gained a position of the highest rank on a worldwide
scale. But most analysts would agree that for science at large this
status was gained either just before or just after World War II.
Some sociologists would set the date earlier, basing their judgments
on such factors as the number of pages published (in books and
journals) and the number of European citations of American publications. But a study of content would yield a somewhat different
picture. Even the Nobel Prizes awarded to Americans prior to
World War II tended to be for new instruments, particular experiments, or new techniques and special effects, and these laureates
were not the men who had created the great overarching theories
and concepts that revolutionized all of science. This opinion is
especially backed up by the personal insights and individual experiences of scientists who were then making their mark. Thus, I.I.
Rabi, the Columbia University physicist and Nobel laureate, went
to study in Germany in the early thirties. At Hamburg, in the physics library, he asked if there was a subscription to the American
Physical Review. The reply was in the affirmative, but he was told
that there were no current issues available; the journal was held in
such low esteem that the library did not receive the journal month
by month, but waited till the end of the year, when a single bound
volume could be put on the library shelf for archival purposes.†

One final word about the state of American science before the

---

* In 1967, federal R&D expenditures were allocated as follows: DOD 43
percent, NACA & NASA 32 percent, AEC 9.5 percent, HEW 7 percent, NSF
1.7 percent.

† Rabi relates that before he went on a postdoctoral trip to Europe, he had
never really come upon a first-rate mind in the sciences. "And there in Hamburg I was close to the greatest minds of the time. Yet I discovered that I

1930's. Our National Academy of Science, founded in 1863, did not have a building of its own, a true home, until the mid-twenties. The foreign secretary complained that there was not even a place available for the storage of the publications of foreign academies which the National Academy received by exchange.

It should thus be fairly obvious that there was a decided break in continuity that occurred just before or after World War II, and that there are no easy historic precedents for a national science policy or for an appreciation by the citizenry at large of the nature and potentialities of science. Nor did American science itself gradually develop its own institutions for dealing adequately with the major problems of science and government, science and social goals and social needs, or even for the adequate organization of its own internal development. Before I address myself to some aspects of these latter problems, a few words are in order about the historical role of science in America.

Whoever contemplates the modest estate of science in our country, in the decades prior to World War II, cannot help but ask why science never came to be a major force in American life and thought during the first century and a half of our nationhood. And such a question must all the more naturally arise when we consider the high place that science held in the hearts and minds of the Founding Fathers of our country, and when we take cognizance of some of the major contributions made to scientific thought and practice by Americans during the colonial period.

It was in America in the eighteenth century that the first public test was made of the newly revealed method of gaining immunity to smallpox: inoculation or variolation. What is most significant

---

knew a lot more physics than the Germans of my age and training — fresh Ph.D.'s. I knew a lot of physics, but I would describe my knowledge by saying I had the libretto without the score. In other words, I was not yet immersed in the living tradition of physics. A lot of what you really accomplish in physics depends upon your taste in what to work on and what to be interested in. You can work very hard on an unimportant problem and show tremendous skill and ingenuity. Before I went to Europe, I had never met real producers of physics. And such physics, and at such a time! It was the most formative experience I had." It is not clear how typical Rabi's experience was, and there can be no doubt that American scientists who had gained their Ph.D.'s were well trained. But they had not yet been in the same continuous contact with the living traditions of research that characterized their fellow students at the same level in Europe. For further information see the "profile" of Rabi, by Jeremy Bernstein, in the *New Yorker,* 13 Oct. 1975, and 20 Oct. 1975.

about this event is that it apparently was the first time that a preventive public health measure was reported in statistical terms, the chances of death from inoculation being compared with the chances of death from smallpox contracted in the normal way.

Colonial Americans provided the first evidence of natural hybridization in plants, and incidentally established the value of using corn (maize) for experiments in plant genetics. Two of the three codiscoverers of Mendel's laws of genetics (in 1899) used corn in their experiments. The significance of the American demonstrations of plant hybridization was that they provided firm evidence in support of the theory that plants reproduce sexually, which became the basis of Linnaeus' comprehensive binomial system of plant classification.

And it was from America that there arose the first general and workable unitary theory of electrical action—a theory that made of electricity a true science, rather than a mere congeries of bizarre and inexplicable individual phenomena—as the French naturalist Buffon described this subject just before Franklin had formulated his general theory. I shall have more to say of Franklin as a scientist in a moment, but here it shall suffice to remark that his theory and his experiments won him a degree of international renown attained by few scientists of the eighteenth century. His book, entitled *Experiments and Observations on Electricity, Made in Philadelphia,* was published in England in five editions during his lifetime; it was speedily translated into French, in which language it went through three editions; and it was published in German and in Italian, and even translated into Latin. In the number of languages in which it was published, and the number of editions, Franklin's book by far surpassed Newton's *Principia* and Newton's *Opticks.* Franklin was elected a fellow of the Royal Society (and forgiven payment of his dues, an honor given to only one other fellow, Isaac Newton) and was awarded the Society's Copley Medal. In 1773 he was elected a "foreign associate" of the French Academy of Sciences, a great honor indeed; by the statutes of the Academy, only eight such foreigners could hold this title at any one time. Incidentally, no American again won this coveted scientific distinction for a hundred years, when Louis Agassiz became a "foreign associate"—but, be it noted, for work that he had done in Europe before emigrating to America.

Two hundred years ago, at the time of the Declaration of Independence, science occupied a prominent place in any roster of values. For the English-speaking world, as for the world of the

French Enlightenment (which set so high a stock on English values), science meant the system of natural philosophy expounded by (or associated with) Isaac Newton, and also the methodological precepts of Francis Bacon. The third member of that British intellectual triumvirate, John Locke, was not only the spokesman for British empiricism and a common-sense philosophy, and the primary authority on the theory of government by "compact" or mutual consent of the governed; he was also the philosophic expositor of the Newtonian doctrines, and he assigned a high place to Newtonian science in his doctrines of education. When Thomas Jefferson wanted three inspirational portraits to adorn his walls he commissioned them to be made of Newton, Locke, and Bacon, and would point to these three as his "trinity of the three greatest men that had ever lived, without any exception, and as having laid the foundation of those superstructures which have been raised in the physical and moral sciences." One of Jefferson's proud possessions was a death mask of Isaac Newton.

The Founding Fathers could not help but be imbued with Newtonian science. John Adams studied this subject while an undergraduate at Harvard College. In his defense of the American constitutions, Adams cited Isaac Newton as an authority when discussing the best form of constitutional government. Arguing against Franklin's desire for a unicameral or single-assembly system with direct election of representatives, Adams remarked:

> The president of Pennsylvania might, upon such an occasion, have recollected one of Sir Isaac Newton's laws of motion, namely. —"that reaction must always be equal and contrary to action," or there can never be any *rest*.

This remark by Adams has been quoted more than once, but—so far as I know—no one has as yet pointed out that Adams had either forgotten what good Professor John Winthrop had taught him at Harvard, or had never really understood the third law. For what Newton had said is that whenever a body A exerts a force on body B, that body B must exert an equal and opposite force on body A. This has nothing whatever to do with rest or equilibrium, which results from a balance of equal and opposite forces on a single body, say A or B.

Franklin's devotion to Newtonian principles is evident to any critical reader of his scientific writings. His guide in the art of experiment was Newton's *Opticks,* and it was from Newton's writings on the aether that Franklin drew his model of the "electric fluid," the basis of his theory of electrical action. His major contribution, in my opinion (and that of his scientific contemporaries), was the principle of conservation of charge. Like the law of conservation or momentum in Newtonian dynamics, Franklin's law of conservation of charge has withstood the test of time; there has never been found an experimental instance of a failure of these two fundamental conservation laws, nor would any theory that violated these laws be considered acceptable today. It is hardly surprising that Franklin the scientist would have thought in the fashion of an experimental physicist in the political realm.

A third major Founding Father, Thomas Jefferson, also had the instincts of a scientist, exhibiting special gifts for ethnology, archaeology, paleontology, and natural history. He was not only president of the United States, but also president of America's oldest scientific organization, the American Philosophical Society. Jefferson's science served his country in important ways on at least two different occasions. One was in the course of a controversy as to whether forms of life (animal, plant, and even human) suffered a kind of "degeneration" in the New World. This theory was particularly expounded by the Abbé Raynal and was supported by Buffon and many other scientists, notably in France. According to its precepts, every species that existed in both the Old and the New Worlds was inferior or "degenerate" in the New. Jefferson fought this theory with evidence based on his own firsthand experience with the aborigines of his native land, and of the fauna and flora he had observed. He not only described the large animals of America; he sent actual specimens, such as the skin and skeleton of a moose, to confute the proponents of this alleged New World "degeneration." A collection of mastodon bones, assembled by Jefferson, is still preserved in the Muséum in Paris, convincing evidence of the giant races that had at one time inhabited North America. A second scientific service was performed by Jefferson in his instructions to Lewis and Clark as to what they should observe and report on during their exploration of the Louisiana Purchase.

Jefferson had an obvious devotion to Newton and the Newtonian scientific enlightenment. He had studied the Newtonian natural philosophy with William Small, a British scientist who had emigrated to America and who became Jefferson's tutor. From the catalogue of Jefferson's library, we may see that he owned the major works of Newton and also those of the chief expositors and commentators, plus the best textbooks of Newtonian physics. In 1814, he ordered from England "a copy of an edition of Newton's *Principia,* which I had seen advertised," the second edition of Motte's English translation, with a supplement by John Machin. In his discussion of a standard of length, based on the length of a seconds pendulum, Jefferson went back to calculations of Isaac Newton, thus giving evidence of his comprehension of Newton's work on the relation between pendulum length and terrestrial latitude; and he adopted Newton's method and results for the "estimate of 39.149 [I]nches for our northern limit of 45°," and also the "difference between the pendulum for 48°51' [the latitude of Paris] and 45°." Jefferson's knowledge on this point was exact and detailed. On other occasions, Jefferson showed himself to be a master of the Newtonian theory of light and explanation of the formation of the rainbow.*

Jefferson's Declaration of Independence shows a decided influence of the special Newtonian aspect of the rationalist Enlightenment philosophy. Recall the stirring opening lines:

> When in the course of human events it becomes necessary for one people to dissolve the political bands which have connected them with another, & to assume among the powers of the earth the separate & equal station, to which the laws of nature & of nature's god entitle them, a decent respect to the opinions of mankind requires that they should declare the causes which impel them to the separation.

Apart from the magnificence of the style, with its felicitous expressions and stately cadences, we cannot help being struck by Jefferson's references to "the laws of nature" and "of nature's god." In this expression of Enlightenment philosophy, with its characteristically eighteenth-century reference to a secular rather than a de-

---

* Scientifically trained readers will be, perhaps, even more impressed by Jefferson's remarks about Lagrange's *Mechanique analytique,* which he had encountered in Paris. It is "a remarkable book," Jefferson wrote, and its author "is allowed to be the greatest mathematician now living, and his personal worth is equal to his science." As to the book itself, let me quote Jefferson's comments in full: "The object of his work is to reduce all the principles of mechanics to the single one of the equilibrium, and to give a simple formula applicable to them all. The subject is treated in the algebraic method, without diagrams to assist the conception." Could any statesman of our own days give so admirable, accurate, and precise a description of an equally technical work? I doubt it.

nominational god, Jefferson has specified in particular the natural order of the universe as revealed by the Newtonian philosophy, in which every planet and indeed every object has its proper place, maintained in a system of utmost stability, despite perturbations, precessions and nutations of axes. This system was the object of constant disquisition in the half-century between Newton's death and the writing of the Declaration.

To the historian of science, however, there is in this opening paragraph a yet more interesting phrase than "nature's god." It is "the laws of nature." Many historians have remarked that Jefferson was fully familiar with the philosophy and indeed the writings of John Locke, Vattel, and such other commentators on natural law as Burlmaqui. And there can be no doubt that the natural law philosophy and the compact theory of government of John Locke were extremely important influences on the philosophy of the Declaration of Independence; they would, no doubt, have been a feature of that document even if it had been written by some other members of the committee of five to whom it had been entrusted by the Continental Congress, for instance, John Adams. This natural law philosophy was especially part and parcel of the intellectual furniture of lawyers, and John Adams was a lawyer.

But Jefferson does not use the common phrase "natural law"— he says specifically and unambiguously, and he does so in all versions and rough drafts, "the laws of nature." The difference may seem to be trivial, but in fact it is not. For, whereas "natural law" or "nature's law" are traditional expressions of a political and social philosophy, and were well recognized as such, the specific phrase "the laws of nature" arises directly in the sciences and specifically in the science of dynamics.

In the discussions of the Constitution, and even in the concept that it might undergo amendment in the light of experience, there is much use of the language of "experiment." In context, however, it is clear that by "experiment" these men by and large were not thinking in scientific terms but rather using this word as synonymous with trial and error, which is not the method of science at all. One must make a distinction, therefore, between the use of this word by the educated laymen among the Founding Fathers and a scientist like Benjamin Franklin. When Franklin wrote in 1786, "We are, I think, in the right road of improvement, for we are making experiments," he was conceiving of experiments in the way that scientists then did. And, when he said in 1788 that it had been decided to follow a policy of "making *experiments* in politics," so that "what knowledge we shall gain by them will be more certain, though perhaps we may hazard too much in *that* mode of acquiring it," Franklin knew perfectly well just what an experiment was. His famous book (cited earlier) began with the words *Experiments and Observations.* As his friend Joseph Priestley (one of the chief expositors of the Franklinian theory of electricity) put it, an experiment is always performed to test a particular hypothesis or question. But most of the men who wrote about the Constitution in Franklin's day were using the word not in the specific scientific sense that Franklin understood, but rather as we do today when we talk about a new type of education or instruction as "experimental," not necessarily implying that we are testing some particular hypothesis, but only trying something new—which may actually be the antithesis of science and all that it stands for.

In their continued use of the word "experiment" in relation to the Constitution and the future of the new nation, most men were actually echoing Hume rather than Newton, and using this word in its traditional sense, expressing its Latin origin: "experiential" or "empirical." But there are some instances in which one may actually detect an overtone of Newtonian rhetoric in the political discussions of that time. Newton had concluded his *Principia* with the statement that he wanted explanations to be based upon sound experimental principles, and that he would "feign no hypotheses"; and then he introduced a discussion of the lack of experiments. In other words, he wished to have an experimental basis for his conclusions, and would not indulge in mere hypotheses or speculations. One cannot help but think of this final statement of Newton's when reading the words of Roger Sherman of Connecticut, ". . . to amend these defects in government, I am not fond of speculation. I would rather proceed on experimental ground." And yet, in context, this too may be no more than Newtonian rhetoric and not an application of the Newtonian natural philosophy, since the "experimental ground" can here be nothing other than simple trial and error. It is not amiss to add that "experience" (and "experiment" in this sense) and its relation to evidence is the natural province of lawyers, and it may be further pointed out that the method of trial and error, and the lessons of experience, are the standbys of successful businessmen, not of scientists.

From what I have said thus far, I hope that two fundamental propositions may emerge. The first is that our eighteenth-century American colonies had produced scientific contributions of real significance, which were acknowledged on a worldwide scale, albeit by a small number of scientists. Second, that prominent political Founding Fathers were familiar with and used the language and rhetoric of Newtonian science, and invoked specific scientific principles, in their discussions of political principles and social philosophy. In short, the intellectual and cultural atmosphere of the founding of our country shows itself to have been, by every test, favorable to the dissemination and cultivation of science.

This feature can be illustrated in many other ways, for instance, by the level of science that was taught in our colonial colleges. In my own Harvard College* we have two striking examples of the importance of science in the education of the young men of those days. When, in 1766, a fire destroyed Harvard Hall, together with the library and its vast collection of scientific apparatus, steps were taken immediately to secure new instruments of science, so that this necessary part of young men's education might not be wanting. During the first year of the Revolution, when Washington's army was quartered in Cambridge, and the teachers and students temporarily withdrew to Watertown, the commencement for that year was delayed, so that the students might have the opportunity to supplement their theoretical scientific learning by contact with the actual apparatus still in Cambridge before getting their degrees. For those who may not be familiar with the incident, may I record that 'the fighting was stopped for three days in 1778, so that the British could allow an expedition of "rebels," organized by the American Academy of Arts and Sciences and Harvard College, to go into enemy territory with their telescopes and clocks in order to observe an eclipse of the sun.

It is well known that the high hopes of the Founding Fathers for the future of science in America were not fulfilled. The history of the American republic during the first century after the Constitution shows itself to have been—with regard to the sciences—just what might have been expected of any other young country. That is, the

---

* Harvard College was not exceptional in its devotion to science during the colonial period. The important place of science in the curriculum of all the colonial colleges has been amply demonstrated.

history during this first century shows no significant effects of the love of science that had characterized so many of the Founding Fathers and that had been so noble a feature of our colonial colleges. One reason may well be that Benjamin Franklin, the foremost scientist of that early period, spent so much of his mature lifetime abroad, and thus did not found a self-perpetuating school of science in America, centered around his own activities. Another significant factor is that the number of practicing scientists in America at the end of the eighteenth century was very small indeed; there seems to be no doubt that in order to establish a self-perpetuating scientific community a certain minimum size is required.*

In this first century, the role of America in the general advancement of the sciences on a worldwide scale was modest. In natural history, and notably in paleontology, there were heroic figures: Rafinesque, Marsh, Cope, Leidy, Say, and others. And such men were not merely observers who just happened to be fortunate enough to be in America where there were new plants, animals, geologic formations, and fossils to be described. They were scientists of quality. But they did not produce profound contributions on a large scale such as we associate with giants like Darwin, Alfred Russell Wallace, Huxley, Claude Bernard, Pasteur, Karl Ernst von Baer, Helmholtz, Julius von Sachs, and so on.

The lack of clear and incisive major contributions to the progress of science may be seen most easily in the domain of physics. Between the time of Franklin in the eighteenth century and that of

---

* A point of view at odds with mine has been developed by Nathan Reingold in a chapter on "American Indifference to Basic Research: A Reappraisal," in *Nineteenth-Century American Science: A Reappraisal,* ed. George Daniels. The opening argument, that "of all Western nations the indifferent Americans devote a greater percentage of their gross national product to research and development in general and probably to basic research in particular," has been somewhat weakened by subsequent events. But Reingold is correct in pointing out that it is easy to magnify the achievements of American colonial science out of context and out of all due proportion, so as to make it appear that there was a nadir in American science between two zeniths: in the eighteenth and twentieth centuries. On the other hand, the general high place given to science (as an ideal for social and political thinking, as a source of intellectual values, as a main subject for education in schools and colleges, and as an area in which research was to be carried out) in the minds of the Founding Fathers and of most political and religious leaders of the late eighteenth century would seem to have opened up a real possibility that the future course of scientific development in our country might have been different from that in the usual developing country—and all the more so in the light of such genuine scientific achievement on the part of Americans.

Willard Gibbs in the later years of the nineteenth, the record in physics shows but one truly significant American contribution, that of Joseph Henry, who had a real talent for electromagnetic science, and was, without question, the ablest physical scientist in America. But he was not in the same class with Ampère, Faraday, Kirchhoff, or Clerk Maxwell.

Physics was not the only science in which, up to the end of the nineteenth century, progress in America was slow. If we look at mathematics before the time of Gibbs, we find a lone significant American innovation of major significance, the "linear associative algebra" of Benjamin Peirce. Yet it is clear that the only true genius in pure mathematics in America in the nineteenth century was J. J. Sylvester, not an American at all, but an Englishman who came to America to teach. In astronomy things appear a little better. At the close of the century America had some of the world's major observatories as well as able astronomers; for example, Newcomb and Pickering. America was the site of early photographic astronomical experiments—the daguerreotype being used in conjunction with a telescope—and important work on the spectral classification of stars was done by Draper. But this was still paltry in comparison with the great research being done in Europe. From American work in chemistry, two contributions were recorded in European annals: Hare's blowtorch and plunge battery and, at the century's end, the work of Josiah Parsons Cooke toward the periodic classification of the chemical elements. How meager this seems when compared with the magisterial achievements of Liebig, Wöhler, Dumas, Pasteur, Berzelius, and Mendeleeff!

In geology, American contributions were greater; at least descriptions of American geological formations made by native scientists were praised by Europeans. And the same is true of the biological sciences to an extent that may somewhat inflate beyond due proportion the reputation of such botanists as John Torrey and Asa Gray.

It is often held that the failure of the young republic to establish a scientific tradition arose from the tendency of Americans to apply rather than to create science. Thus, Tocqueville wrote, "It must be confessed that among the civilized people of our age, there are few in which the sciences have made so little progress as in the United States." Had America been alone in the world, he held, then she would have had to learn that to apply science one must first have

science to apply. As things were, America was merely drawing on
the accumulated scientific resources of Europe without adding anything of her own save the uses to which existing knowledge could
be put. Tocqueville concluded by asking whether "the passion for
profound knowledge, so rare and so fruitful," which had produced
the theoretical European science, could "be born and developed so
readily in democratic societies as in aristocracies." While only the
future could answer the question, he concluded, "As for me, I can
hardly believe it."

The next half-century in the United States seems to have proved
the correctness of Tocqueville's prediction with regard to pure
science, though the record shows a generous overestimate on his part
of the role in America of the applied sciences, at least at the time
of his visit in the 1830's. We must keep in mind, however, that until
almost the end of the nineteenth century, technology and engineering did not in general depend on the applications of pure science,
by which I mean the discovery of new scientific principles. This
was the era of empirical innovation and mechanical invention. And
it is, I believe, clear and beyond argument that in inventiveness
America became a major nation early in the nineteenth century.
Any comparative study of the number of inventions in nineteenth-
century America and other countries (by the crude method of
counting patents) readily shows a greater number made by Americans than by those of any other nationality. A typical major invention was barbed wire (often associated with Glidden's patent of
1874), based on a device for twisting strands of wire with occasional
barbed spurs. The invention of this kind of wire made homestead-
ing possible; in the Great Plains there was no supply of wood or stone
for use in fencing off ploughed land to protect it from cattle. The
reaper, the sewing machine and the Colt revolver are other examples
of this mechanical type of invention, as are improved steamboats
and steam locomotives. Yet as early as the 1840's the applications
of scientific discovery were beginning to be of importance. As types,
may I cite the telegraph and photography—both dependent on
recent discoveries in the pure sciences of physics and chemistry.
From then until now, with constant acceleration for about one
hundred years, America has excelled in the applications of science—
but not necessarily the science she has herself produced.

In the first fifty years of the republic, however, there seems to
have been about as great a want of applied science as of pure sci-

ence. Thus any failure of America to produce a great scientific
tradition by mid-century can hardly be ascribed to a concentration
on application rather than on theory. It was late in the second half
of the nineteenth century, and in the first decades of the twentieth
century—when the pure sciences had at last begun to prosper in
America—that our men of science began to complain of America's
overvaluation of the applications of science with its consequence
that the advancement of knowledge for its own sake aroused little
financial support and intellectual enthusiasm. But, plainly, we must
exercise caution lest we mistakenly ascribe to early nineteenth-
century American science the large-scale industrial and agricultural
practical applications of science that so completely altered the
material conditions of life in the late 1800's and in our own century.

By the mid-1840's the stress on practicality produced schools of
science at both Harvard and Yale in which a dominant theme was
the utility of the sciences. Harvard's Lawrence Scientific School
was founded in 1847 specifically for those men who intended

> to enter upon an active life as engineers or chemists, or, in general,
> as men of science, applying their attainments to practical purposes,
> where they may learn what has been done at other times and in
> other countries. . . .
> Inventive men laboriously re-invent what has been produced
> before. Ignorant men fight against the laws of nature with a vain
> energy, and purchase their experience at great cost. Why should not
> all these start where their predecessors ended, and not where they
> began?

This statement by Abbott Lawrence, about his proposed school at
Harvard, is extraordinarily interesting to the historian, because its
propagandistic tone makes clear that in the late 1840's Americans
had not yet come to a full appreciation of the importance of the
practical applications of science. Special schools already existed
where one could study law, medicine, and surgery; but where, Lawrence asked, "can we send those who intend to devote themselves to
the practical applications of science?" In New Haven, the Sheffield
Scientific School was also formed in the 1840's: the initial steps
being the appointment of John Pitkin Norton as Professor of
Agricultural Chemistry and Animal and Vegetable Physiology, and
of Benjamin Silliman, Jr., as Professor of Practical Chemistry. It
was the latter's specific obligation to give instruction "in respect to
the application of chemistry and the kindred sciences to the man-

ufacturing arts, to the exploration of the resources of the country and to other practical uses."*

The difficulties in establishing a scientific tradition may be seen in the several attempts which were made in the decades following the War of 1812 to establish permanent scientific institutions and organizations. Especially, there were endeavors to form *national* scientific organizations. The failures were in no case wholly complete; each seemingly abortive effort left its residue of experience for the ones that succeeded it. The goal was a permanent national scientific organization, one closely related to the government in a double sense: through the obligation on the part of the government of financial assistance, and through the duty of the scientists to be of service to the government and to give official advice. These successive attempts were without success; and it was not until 1863 (in the midst of the Civil War) that our National Academy of Sciences was finally established. The successive failures either to interest the federal government in supporting a program of scientific research, or to obtain federal sanction for a truly national academy of sciences, were in some measure related to the great debate concerning states' rights (and the limitations of federal power), and to a fear that had existed since Jefferson's day of establishing aristocratic or monarchial institutions. As a result, the first national scientific establishment within the government was the Smithsonian Institution, which was supported by private funds willed to the United States by an Englishman.

As has just been mentioned, there was no national academy of sciences in our country until Civil War days. Organized when the national pattern of life was already well established, the National Academy of Sciences in its first half-century never played the major role either in national affairs or in organized American science that characterized its European counterparts. Although formed in time of war, in part to serve as official adviser to the government, the Academy—from the end of the Civil War to the near close of the century—was rarely called upon for such service, and not in any major way. As late as 1902, the Academy's want of even a permanent headquarters with library and rooms for meetings or con-

---

* The new department at Yale called itself the School of Applied Chemistry; it combined with the School of Engineering in 1851 to become the Yale Scientific School, later (in 1861) renamed the Sheffield Scientific School in honor of a benefactor.

ferences was cited among the conditions which discourage scientific
work in America.

In the decades following the Civil War, a number of new features are discernible in the American scientific scene. One of these
is the rise of agricultural research. In 1862 a full-scale department
was established. But it was not until a decade later that the scientific
work of the Department of Agriculture grew and expanded, accompanied by the rise of state agricultural experiment stations. The
latter were aided by the Morrill Act and even more substantially
and directly by the Hatch Act of 1887.

By the 1860's scientific work was being conducted not only in
the Department of Agriculture, but also in the Coast Survey (which
had an abortive start in the days of Jefferson, then a rebirth under
its Swiss-American founder Hassler, and at last a new career under
the guiding hands of Alexander Dallas Bache). The federal government authorized G. W. Featherstonhaugh in 1834, under the direction of the War Department, to make a geological and mineralogical
survey of the Ozark Mountain region. In 1830 the first state geological survey was undertaken by Massachusetts, and within ten
years there were sixteen others. A national observatory had been
established—although without direct sanction—in 1842, when provision was made for a permanent depot of charts and instruments
for the Navy. Astronomical observations were begun in 1845, and
within three years the depot was designated the Naval Observatory,
which name it still bears.

Thus, by the end of the Civil War, scientific work was being done
within the federal government by the Smithsonian Institution, the
Coast Survey, the Naval Observatory, and the Department of Agriculture. The way was open for that expansion of bureaus with
scientific concerns which became characteristic of late nineteenth-
century America. By 1884 science within the government had assumed proportions of such magnitude and complexity that a joint
commission of the Congress (known generally as the Allison Commission, for its chairman, Senator W. B. Allison) was appointed to
study the existing organization of a number of federal agencies concerned with science in an attempt "to secure greater efficiency and
economy of administration in the public service." In the end, no
action was taken on the commission's proposals for reorganization,
stemming from a report prepared by the National Academy of
Sciences. Neither congressmen nor senators were much moved by

the Academy's conclusion that "none who have ever lived with open eyes during the development of these results of purely scientific investigations doubt that the cultivation of science 'promotes the general welfare.' "

The era following the Civil War witnessed the growth of applied science and the beginning of industrial scientific research. It was the time of the founding of scientific schools and the development of polytechnic institutes on the European model, including special institutions for roads and bridges, mines, forestry, and so on. Engineering schools already existed at Rensselaer and West Point, and there were the Sheffield and Lawrence scientific schools. The Massachusetts Institute of Technology was established in 1861; by 1899 there were 2,000 graduates. In 1864 Columbia had a school of mines that came to embrace chemistry, civil engineering, sanitary engineering and architecture. In 1868 the Worcester Polytechnic Institute was founded on a model of similar schools in Moscow and St. Petersburg. Other engineering schools established before 1900 include Lehigh, Stevens Institute of Technology (Hoboken), Case School of Applied Science (Cleveland), Rose Polytechnic Institute (Terre Haute), Throop Polytechnic Institute (now California Institute of Technology at Pasadena), and Armour Institute (now the Illinois Institute of Technology, Chicago). At the same time, major scientific schools had grown up at Princeton, Columbia, Pennsylvania, Dartmouth, and Rutgers, and the scientific departments had become more and more important in other colleges and universities, notably such state universities as Michigan and Wisconsin.

It is difficult today to believe that the community of American scientists was so very small a century ago. In 1860 the American Association for the Advancement of Science could boast of only 644 members, a figure which dropped because of the Civil War and rose again only to 536 by 1870. Although the membership of the AAAS included many doctors, clergymen, teachers and laymen interested in science, who were not scientists at all, the rolls did not even pass the 2,000 mark by 1900. One can easily imagine, therefore, the great concern of American men of science for the improvement of both the quantity and quality of the scientific movement in the United States. In 1872 twenty-five frustrated American scientists began a movement to improve the state of American science by inviting to our shores one of England's most renowned lecturers

on science, John Tyndall. The group was led by Joseph Henry and
Edward Livingston Youmans, then editor of the *Popular Science
Monthly* and one of the great propagandists for science in America
in this period. Tyndall had been invited to America on the specific
ground that "a course of experimental lectures would materially
promote scientific education" in the United States. Tyndall's success shows that there was a great popular interest in scientific subjects. He gave six lectures in Boston, in Philadelphia, in Washington,
in New York, and in Brooklyn; he gave two lectures in New Haven
and three in Baltimore. After four months, he found himself the
richer by $23,100, and was embarrassed to have made such a profit.
Before his departure, Tyndall announced that he was not going to
take the money back to England with him, since the purpose of his
visit had not been for his own pecuniary advantage. He therefore
left the "surplus above expenses" in trust for the advancement of
science in America, the interest to be expended "in aid of students
who devote themselves to original researches." Many eminent physicists have been "Tyndall Fellows." The first was Michael Pupin,
who has left for us in his autobiography, *From Immigrant to Inven-
tor,* a dramatic and thrilling account of his adventures in becoming
a scientist in America.

At the farewell banquet given in his honor at Delmonico's in
New York, on February 4, 1873, Tyndall analyzed the American
scientific scene. He was disturbed by the emphasis on applications
of science rather than the cultivation of science "for its own sake,
for the pure love of truth, rather than for the applause or profit it
brings." He recommended that America honor the men whose research created new ideas as well as those who devised new things or
new ways of making or doing things. He urged the founding of
chairs "which shall have original research for their main object and
ambition." Above all, he warned against the evils of the scientist
seeking public acclaim, of the "investigator who is fond of wander-
ing from his true vocation to appear on public platforms." These
remarks underline the low position of the original investigator in
America at that time; his academic advancement did not in any
way depend on the success or significance of original research.

From the time of the Civil War to the end of the century the
applications of science to industry, agriculture, medicine and communication were definitely a part of the national scene. This emphasis on practice, even in the old established colleges, may be seen

most clearly in the early career of J. Willard Gibbs, whose eventual contribution to pure science was of so abstract a nature that few of his countrymen could understand his publications, much less see their profound significance and long-range effects on both theory and practice.

Gibbs's work in thermodynamics, vector analysis and statistical mechanics is at the foundation of modern theoretical physics and chemistry; he is one of the greatest scientists that America has ever brought forth. Gibbs earned his Ph.D. at Yale in 1863, the third year in which that degree was offered. His unusual talent in mathematics led him—naturally enough for those days—to a career in engineering. The subject of his thesis was the design of gears, and he invented a "center vent" hydraulic turbine and a railroad brake (patented in 1866) which had some rather extraordinary features in that it worked whether the train was going forward or backward and whether the locomotive was at the front or the rear end of the train. He also wrote a work on governors for steam engines.

Not satisfied with his education, and wanting to learn more mathematics and physics, young Gibbs went abroad to study. In Paris and in Berlin he came under the influence of such men as Magnus, Weierstrass, Darboux, Chasles, Duhamel, and Liouville. The notebooks that Gibbs kept during this period show a shift in interest from steam-engine governors and railway brakes to pure mathematics and mathematical physics. He returned to America, devoting himself to these latter two subjects, and his career was thenceforth marked by contributions to abstract or pure science, but not to engineering. In 1871 he became professor of mathematical physics at Yale, and it is another reflection on the times that such a man was paid no salary.*

The failure of America to produce a just share of pure science and the overemphasis on applied science may be seen again and again as a topic in the writings of American men of science in the

---

* He was offered a post at Bowdoin in 1873, and later at Johns Hopkins in 1879; so that it cannot be said that Gibbs was wholly without reputation in America. J. J. Thomson later recalled the visit of a newly elected president of an American university who wanted to find a professor of molecular physics. Thomson recommended Willard Gibbs, only to be told that he probably had intended to mention Wolcott Gibbs, who was a chemist at Harvard (a very able man, though not in the same category as Willard). "No," replied J. J. Thomson, "I mean Willard Gibbs." The visitor asked for another name, saying: "Willard Gibbs can't be a man of much personal magnetism or I should have heard of him."

late nineteenth century. In an editorial written in 1883 for the
first issue of *Science* (now the official weekly journal of the American Association for the Advancement of Science), it was stated
without equivocation:

> The leading feature of American science, however, and that
> which most distinctively characterizes it, is its utilitarianism. True,
> there are in our country able investigators working in scientific fields
> which do not offer the promise of material reward; but notwith-
> standing this, it remains still true that those sciences whose prin-
> ciples are capable of useful application are the most zealously culti-
> vated among us, and attract the largest number of students. . . .
> Nor is this to be at all regretted. Research is none the less genuine,
> investigation none the less worthy, because the truth it discovers is
> utilizable for the benefit of mankind. Granting, even, that the dis-
> covery of truth for its own sake is a nobler pursuit, because a less
> purely selfish one; does it become any the less noble when it is
> ascertained that the truth thus discovered is capable of important
> applications which increase tenfold the happiness of human life?

What did it matter, then, that we could not "boast of a scientific
record as full and complete as that of other countries"?

Although the close of the nineteenth century was characterized
by the expansion of colleges and universities, the inauguration of
graduate schools on continental models, and the founding of engineering and technical institutes, these centers of higher education
did not at that time become firmly established as the homes of dis-
interested scientific research. There are at least two apparent causes
for this situation. One is the relatively low estate in which college
and university teachers found themselves. Another is the tradition
of young men choosing a college without reference to the original
contributions to knowledge of the individuals comprising the faculty.
These aspects of American science were stressed in two articles
which Simon Newcomb, the astronomer, one of the distinguished
scientists in America in the nineteenth century, wrote for the *North
American Review*. In the first of these, published in 1874, called,
"Exact Science in America," Newcomb expressed his deep concern
that Americans, despite their faith in the "future greatness of their
country," had an opinion of its "intellectual development [which]
is modest in the extreme." All that Americans have learned, according to Newcomb, led them to believe that first-rate men of science
are necessarily of transatlantic origin. Not only did Newcomb find
this belief widespread, but he found also that the American citizen

had "a theory which explains the deficiency to his entire satisfaction, and, indeed, reconciles him to it, namely, that the activities and energies of this country are all directed toward material development, and that the atmosphere produced by this development is unfavorable to the production of the highest intellectual qualities." But, were we to examine "the applications, we should find our country in the front ranks of progress."

Searching for possible causes of America's low scientific state, Newcomb called particular attention to "the relative inducements to scientific research here and in Europe." He found that, unlike his European counterpart, the American professor did not have to demonstrate a talent for research in order to become eminent among either his colleagues or the public at large. This American professor was described by Newcomb as follows:

> Among the large number of our so-called universities, in fact at all outside of the Eastern States, nothing more is expected of a professor than acquaintance with a certain defined curriculum, and ability to carry the student through it. . . . However great the knowledge of the subject which may be expected in a professor, he is not for a moment expected to be an original investigator, and the labor of becoming such, so far as his professional position is concerned, is entirely gratuitous.

In short,

> The various deficiencies in the incentives to scientific research which we have described may be summed up in the single proposition, that the American public has no adequate appreciation of the superiority of original research to simple knowledge. It is too prone to look upon great intellectual efforts as mere *tours de force,* worthy of more admiration than the feats of the gymnast, but not half so amusing, and no more in need of public support.

Thus Newcomb deplored the fact that many Americans made a scientific reputation not so much for having done significant original research as for having had success at popularization.*

---

* In 1883, in *Science,* an editorial on "National Traits in Science" ended with this paragraph: "America's contributions to pure sciences are by no means very extensive, or often very important: compared with the great volume of German production they seem almost insignificant. We have never duly fostered research, for we have bestowed upon it neither the proper esteem nor office. There are, we suppose, at least six thousand 'professors' in the United States: are one hundred and fifty of them active investigators? The time

In 1883, Henry A. Rowland entitled his address as vice-president of the American Association for the Advancement of Science "A Plea for Pure Science." Rowland, professor at Johns Hopkins and at that time America's only experimental physicist of established first rank, told his audience quite frankly that "American science is a thing of the future, and not of the present or past." Chief among the causes of this condition he placed the confusion between pure science and its applications. Another reason he found was the lack of concentration of scientific resources. As an example, he cited the growing number of well-equipped observatories, yet each lacking sufficient endowment or other financial support to maintain adequate research staffs. Spreading the scientific resources of the nation thinly could result only in "mediocrity," he believed, a mediocrity which he found to be the "curse" of America. A decade and a half later, in 1899, Rowland returned to these subjects in his presidential address at the New York meeting of the newly founded American Physical Society; his subject was "The Highest Aim of the Physicist." Alas, he said, he must decry the fact that the condition of American science was in many ways as bad as he had found it "fifteen years ago . . . much of the intellect of the country is still wasted in the pursuit of the so-called practical science which ministers to our physical needs and but little thought and money are given to the grander portion of the subject which appeals to our intellect alone."*

There were signs, however, that the situation was improving. Rowland in 1899 referred to the "experiment of Michelson to detect the etherial wind" which "failed to detect any relative motion of the matter and the ether"; of course, he could not know that this

---

seems remote when every American professor will be expected to be also an investigator; but among us is a little band of men who have before them the model of Germany, and who are working earnestly for the intellectual elevation of their country. Their first object is necessarily to render research more important in public estimation, and so to smooth the way for a corps of professional investigators. Every thoughtful person must wish success to the attempt."

* America's attitude toward research may be illustrated by the case of Ira Remsen, the inaugural professor of chemistry at the first institution to be established in America for postgraduate work: the Johns Hopkins University. Remsen had been trained in Europe, receiving his Ph.D. at Göttingen in 1870. He became professor at Williams College in 1872. There he found no laboratory. When he requested one, the reply of the president was: "You will please keep in mind that this is a college and not a technical school. The students who come here are not to be trained as chemists or geologists or physicists. They are to be taught the great fundamental truths of all sciences. The object aimed at is culture, not practical knowledge." Remsen later recalled a faculty

experiment—performed in concert with Morley—was to become one of the most famous experiments of all time and thus bring true renown to American exact science. In 1875 the Johns Hopkins University had been founded, an event of enormous consequence to science and to all American higher learning, because this university—established firmly on continental European models—was dedicated to advanced training and research and set a standard to be followed by other institutions. Gifts of private capital had begun to endow great instruments of research, notably in astronomy (e.g., the Lick and Yerkes observatories), and it was becoming clear that adequate finances would be available to support research in other areas too. One of the major needs of American science was adequate financing of both professors and students. In an analysis made in 1892, Addison Brown found that in the whole of the United States there were but twenty-six "adequately endowed postgraduate fellowships in science." Since a student required three years of postgraduate study to become a full-fledged scientist, there was provision for only nine such students a year. No wonder that America was not yet producing her quota of scientists!

By the beginning of the twentieth century the gloomy picture did show some signs of better days ahead. In 1901, just two years after Rowland's address to the physicists, Theodore W. Richards of Harvard, a native American chemist, achieved the then unheard-of distinction of being offered a regular professorship in a German university, Göttingen. He refused, however, and built his career in his native country. He set the seal on the growing scientific eminence of America by winning the Nobel Prize in chemistry—the second such award to be won by an American scientist, the first having been gained by A. A. Michelson in physics.

By the time of World War I, American science had certainly achieved a respectable position in the world scene, but had not yet reached a level of greatness commensurate with the size and strength to which America had grown. The day was still far off when an American scientist could consider himself well prepared for research

---

meeting held in the college library. One of his articles had just been published in the *American Journal of Science*. Someone picked up the number and tried without success to read the title aloud; then followed some "good-natured fun." Said Remsen, "I felt that in the eyes of my colleagues I was rather a ridiculous subject." This story, typical of the period, indicates that scientific research and knowledge were clearly not considered to be very important in American higher education.

without a period of training in Europe, and a still longer time would have to pass before it would become generally customary for Europeans to desire similar training in America as the necessary condition for becoming successful investigators.

Undoubtedly, the failure of the scientist to achieve the same place in nineteenth-century American cultural life as his European counterpart is related to the more general situation of intellectuals and particularly of college professors. The history of the sciences in nineteenth-century America also demonstrates one of the special aspects of science as an enterprise. The establishment of a scientific tradition, it would appear, requires more than the production of able individual scientists. There is needed a group of men working in either loose or close association, attracting still others who are fired by the pride of continuing, extending, revising, and perhaps in the end finding substitutes for the original concepts, experiments, or procedures. Such a level of activity, given financial support and intellectual respectability, perpetuates itself and may even incite similar activity in other fields. In this sense the failure of American science in the nineteenth century was not so much the lack of individual men of high order as the failure to achieve the conditions under which a true scientific tradition could become established at all.

In the years following World War I, American science gained constantly in respectability and power. In certain fields—such as genetics and other branches of biology and the biomedical sciences and some branches of astronomy—America produced science on as high a level as anywhere in Europe. And yet the flow of students continued to be eastward across the Atlantic throughout the twenties. These students tended to come back fired with enthusiasm to produce a science in their own countries that would be the equal of any in the world. Thus it was that in the early thirties the status of American science was already on the rise, and the ground was prepared for the great influx of scientific talent that occurred in the late thirties and that was to become so important in America's meteoric rise to the extraordinary scientific eminence of the forties and fifties, continuing through the sixties and seventies.

The National Academy of Sciences was founded as noted above during the Civil War. It has had a curious history, one that actually both reflects the impracticality of the terms of its foundation and the low estate of science in the United States prior to World War II.

For the Academy was to be (and is) both an honorary society, self-perpetuating, whose members are chosen for their eminence within their fields of specialization, and also an organization of experts with the express mission of serving the government as a chief scientific advisory body. These two aims or functions tend to be incompatible, since the soundest adviser on practical questions of national policy is not necessarily the outstanding academic scientist working in that area. And, indeed, in the years following World War I most of the hard work done by the Academy was commissioned through a daughter organization, the National Research Council, whose members were chosen for their competence to undertake a particular assignment, rather than for their academic eminence. The National Research Council was created by the Academy during the First World War, when it became apparent that the Academy itself could not effectively mobilize America's scientific manpower for the needs of war. During the first half-century of the Academy's existence, more than one-third of the committees appointed to serve the government were responses to calls made during the first five years of the Academy's existence (which includes the Civil War period). The Academy's history until the 1940's, when it came to life as a side effect of the rise in national importance of American science, provides eloquent testimony to the fact that our national political system had developed without a place in it for science.

I have referred, at the beginning of this paper, to certain signs and evidence that our country had become a major scientific nation by the 1960's and early 1970's. But there are, in my opinion, good grounds for concern as to the future. The magic figure of 3 percent of the GNP spent in America for scientific R&D in 1964, the envy of the rest of the world, had slipped down to but 2.6 percent by 1971, and was surpassed by an estimated 3 percent in the USSR.* Again, by 1971, the number of scientists and engineers engaged in R&D per 10,000 population began to decrease after 1969 in the U.S., al-

---

* In the U.K. and W. Germany, this figure was about 2 percent, and in Japan and France 1.8 percent.

The decline may be seen in other ways, as follows: our "national expenditures for R&D—expressed in constant 1958 dollars—declined 6 percent between 1968 and 1971. Total R&D expenditures as a proportion of the GNP declined to 2.5 percent in 1972 from a high of 3 percent in 1964. The number of scientists and engineers engaged in R&D reached a peak of almost 560,000 in 1969 and declined each year thereafter for a total reduction of 35,000 by 1972. Federal funds for industrial R&D declined in current dollars

though the number increased in the USSR, Japan, West Germany and France. In 1971, this number was 37 per 10,000 population in the USSR, but only 25 per 10,000 population in the U.S.* It should be noted, however, that the scientific literature originating in the U.S. was still being cited in 1971 more frequently than that of any other country in physics and geophysics, chemistry and metallurgy, molecular biology, engineering, psychology, and economics. But on this level of citation indexes, whatever they may mean, the U.K. stood first in mathematics and in systematic biology.†

In days ahead, will the stringencies of a shrinking budget be felt most in science's most sensitive area, basic research? How can a congressman easily give support to an intellectual pursuit, the very titles of which (as announced in any list of grants awarded) are too frequently unpronounceable and not understandable? How will a congressman justify such expenditures to a skeptical constituency? The National Science Foundation, America's primary agency supporting basic research or fundamental science, has come increasingly under fire for the abstruse or even seemingly ridiculous nature of some of the projects it supports. It has even been seriously proposed that a list of all proposed projects, big or small, should have to be submitted to the Congress before being funded, so that any project that might offend or appear ridiculous to any congressman could then be vetoed and eliminated. Particularly offensive to many

---

after 1969. And the fraction of Federal outlays devoted to R&D fell from 12 to 7 percent between 1965 and 1972. As of 1972, 73 percent of all Federal R&D expenditures went for national defense and space and only 27 percent for civilian needs.

"The impact of these indicators can best be seen in the slow rate of growth in U.S. productivity. Thus U.S. productivity gained only 39 percent over the last decade compared to 210 percent for Japan, 86 percent for West Germany, 81 percent for France, and 50 percent for the United Kingdom. And from 1966 to 1971, productivity gains in the United States were outpaced by increasing labor costs." (Quoted from a statement on national science policy and priorities, U.S. Senate, 11 Oct. 1974, by Senator Edward M. Kennedy.)

* Some corresponding numbers are 25 Japan (same as U.S.), 15 West Germany, 12 France.

† An independent study in 1974 by Pierre Aigrain, former delegate for scientific and technical development in France (a post equivalent to that of our presidential science adviser plus certain power in allocating funds which we vest in the Office of Management and Budget), showed a marked decline over 10 years in U.S. commitment to scientific research and development, especially in comparison with the Western European countries and Japan. But, he noted, the U.S. was still ahead of these countries in "percentage of its gross national product allocated to research and development and percentage of manpower working" in pure and applied science and development.

of our elected representatives is the fact that research grants for basic science are given largely on merit, on the basis of a "peer-review" system; this puts the granting of funds, so it is alleged, into the hands of an "old-boy network," with the result that "to him who hath, shall be given." That is, these funds go in large quantities to centers of excellence, located in New England and the central Atlantic states, in a few North Central states, and California, whereas it is generally considered that the federal pie should be cut up more evenly among the several states.

In these discussions there is exhibited a considerable misunderstanding about the national importance of basic science or fundamental research and the equitable distribution of public funds by states. This kind of uncertainty with respect to science and its public support is directly related, in my opinion, to two historical factors. One is that science at large has become a major concern of government in the U.S. only in the last several decades. The other is a general ignorance among our countrymen as to the nature of science itself, and in particular the relation between advances in knowledge and the applications of scientific knowledge to human affairs. This ignorance is, I believe, itself a result of the fact that our country has only recently attained the status of a first-rate scientific power.

Let me illustrate these points by a few examples. At the end of World War II, America was able to send vast quantities of food to Europe, because of the agricultural surplus. But what is not generally known is that the improvement in a single crop, corn or maize, was so great that the increased yield could account for all the food exported by us in 1945 and 1946. This had come about as a result of the introduction of so-called hybrid corn,* specially bred and hybridized to insure high-yielding, disease-resistant strains. This corn was not—and could not have been—produced by practical men, corn-breeders primarily interested in improving the annual harvest. It came into being because a group of plant scientists were interested in experimental evolution; they inbred common or field (open-pollinated) corn for generation after generation until there resulted a series of pure lines, that is, those that would continue to breed true when fertilized under controlled conditions. Later on, it

---

* All common field corn is hybrid. The difference is that the new corn was the result of a double-cross (A x B) x (B x C) of four of the pure inbred lines that are the ancestors of ordinary corn.

was seen that these pure lines could be recombined according to a breeder's design and so yield corn far superior in a number of characteristics to the open-pollinated field variety.

From the practical man's point of view, these inbred lines got worse and worse, or less and less useful for breeding purposes, with each generation—the final pure lines had ears that were small and scrawny, with very few kernels on each ear, and all too few ears per plant. No practical man would thus ever have continued with these experiments and no ordinarily practical man would have been able to achieve this astonishing increase in agricultural production.

Is is not easy for the nonscientist to comprehend fully the nature of science and—above all—the delicate and complex net or relationships between basic science or fundamental research (what used to be called "pure" science) and applications. The National Science Foundation has established a division known as RANN (Research and National Needs), but it is plain to those in the know that national needs tomorrow may also be served by research that seems today to be so abstruse and abstract that few can comprehend it, much less envision any future usefulness. It is such a program, based on ignorance of science and its ways, that establishes a "war on cancer" and really believes the enemy may be overcome in a single campaign. And it is ignorance of the same kind that is expressed in such statements as, "If science can put a man on the moon, why can't science solve the problems of the city?"

In the tenth annual report of the National Science Foundation, in 1960, Director Allen Waterman sadly observed:

> In the area of scientific research and its extension into development and production there is a growing realization of the importance of continuity and proper apportionment of support through all stages, starting with basic research and extending through applied research, development, and production. However, it is still true that in spite of repeated emphasis upon the importance of basic research, support for this effort has only barely held its own in relation to the larger and seemingly more pressing problems of development. It has proved far more difficult to secure adequate support for basic progress in science than for the applications of science, because of the seeming vagueness of the enterprise, especially when high-priority, costly practical goals have to be met. Vannevar Bush's pithy statement, "Applied research drives out basic," is constantly being verified. If the full potentialities of our society are to be realized, however, we must by all means insure that the frontiers of science are pushed forward energetically.

Today, a decade and a half later, these words still ring true. I would agree, of course, that there is no obvious and easy correlation between a general appreciation of the nature of science and the state of greatness that a nation may attain. But in a country with a government like ours, with its immediate and ready reaction to public sentiment (which follows from a committee system rather than a parliamentary system, and from a free system in which public opinion has true force), the degree of public understanding of science may play a rather crucial role in the future of science through the control of the purse strings.

As an example of the ways in which the sciences themselves, or their major spokesmen, are ignored by our lawmakers, let me refer to some statistics in recent history. As most readers are aware, government agencies draw up their annual projected budgets as a result of the work of staff members (often in consultation with outside experts or representatives of a field). Then the budget is subjected to scrutiny by the Bureau of the Budget (now the Office of Management and Budget), which sets a recommended figure, usually lower, which goes to the Congress. There, it is usually the case that an appropriation is voted in the House at a figure much cut down; next, the Senate is apt to vote an appropriation with the cut restored; and a compromise is then reached by a joint committee. In 1952-53-54, just after the National Science Foundation had been established, there was a statutory limitation of $15 million for the annual budget. In each of these years, NSF asked for either the whole $15 million or a little less, a sum that appeared in the president's budget with the approval of the Bureau of the Budget. As expected, the House allowance was small and the Senate's larger (though well under the amount requested) and the final appropriations for these three fiscal years were, respectively, $3.5 million, $4.7 million, and $8 million. Until 1958, after the ceiling had been lifted, year after year the final appropriation was only from 60 to 68 percent of what the NSF had reckoned to be necessary for the health and growth of the nation's basic science. Then, in 1959, there was a sudden change. NSF's estimate jumped up; and in that year the Congress finally appropriated almost the whole amount requested, $134 million. But the next year, the final appropriation of the Congress was only about two-thirds of what NSF had reckoned its needs to be. A more cautious estimate was accordingly made for fiscal 1961, when the final appropriation of $175 million was some 80 percent of the amount the NSF thought was needed for the accomplishment of its mission.

The otherwise uninformed reader would draw two conclusions from these data. One, that the Congress thought it could make a better judgment concerning the needs of basic science than the scientists or the experts in the National Science Foundation. Two, that there was no question here of the Congress correcting the best judgment of the scientific community; rather, the Congress was simply exercising its customary restraint and parsimony. The Congress, it may be supposed, was merely unwilling to spend all that money on science. A different conclusion results from examining what was happening during those same years to the appropriation requests of the National Institutes of Health, which had assumed the primary responsibility for research in the life sciences. In 1956, when the Congress voted to appropriate only 66 percent of the budget requested for NSF, it ended up by giving NIH more than it had requested by $6 million, just about the same amount that it denied the NSF. And in 1957, the final appropriation to NIH was about 50 percent more than NIH had requested (and probably was 50 percent more than NIH knew what to do with); this excess, this free gift, was in amount $56 million, just about the size of NSF's budgetary estimate for that same year, in which the actual final appropriation was but $40 million. Again, in 1958, the Congress ended up by appropriating to NIH almost $20 million more than it had requested, in a year in which the sum it denied to NSF in the final appropriation was $23 million. In short, the Congress was not simply being parsimonious; rather, it was reordering the priorities of the scientists themselves, giving to NIH what it was denying to NSF.*

In the foregoing bit of financial history, there is another indication of the chancy nature of public support of science in the U.S. The support level for NSF continued at $16 million annually or less during 1954-55-56 (it was $8 million for fiscal 1954, $12.3 million for 1953), and then more than trebled to $40 million for 1957. It remained at that level for two years (being $49.8 million for 1958)

---

* It should be noted that there were many factors involved. The life sciences, with their apparent immediate applicability to health, are far more glamorous than ordinary chemistry, physics, or geology. Then, too, the NIH had extraordinary spokesmen in the Congress in the persons of Senator Hill and Congressman Fogarty, aided and abetted by a powerful lobby led by Mary Lasker and others. As may be expected, the NSF drew back in its support of the life sciences (leaving this area largely to NIH) and concentrated on mathematics, physics, chemistry, astronomy, and the earth sciences.

and then took another tremendous jump to $134 million, an increase over 1957 by almost a factor of 4. Why? The jump in 1957 (from $16 million to $40 million) was a response to the publication of a study by the National Research Council, entitled *Soviet Professional Manpower*. As the Director of NSF wrote in his annual report, this study "drew sobering comparisons between the rates at which the U.S. and the USSR are training scientific and technical manpower," and the increase in the budget of NSF was our response to the Soviet threat. "The next large increment came in 1959 when $134 million was appropriated in the wake of intense national concern over the Russian sputnik and all that it implied."

Another bit of fallout from the Soviet success in launching the first Sputnik was the establishment in 1957 by President Eisenhower of the post of the president's special assistant for science and technology within the president's executive office, together with the President's Science Advisory Committee (PSAC). Eventually, the president's science adviser (as the president's special assistant for science and technology came to be known) became a powerful figure, chairman of PSAC and of both the Office of Science and Technology (1962) and the Federal Council on Science and Technology. He not only attended meetings of the cabinet, but of the National Security Council, the Defense Science Board of the Department of Defense, and even (at times) the meetings of the Joint Chiefs of Staff. Most important, he was described in relation to "an unparalleled means of access to the president, whom he assists directly in all matters of science policy." At last, thanks to the rivalry with the Soviet Union, the scientific community was able to make a creative input in the affairs of state, and to give direct advice to the president on the many diverse problems which were science related.* In fact, as subsequent history was to show, this link between science and the president was only a very tenuous one. For

---

* On 15 October 1957, eleven days after the launching of Sputnik, Professor I. I. Rabi, then chairman of the Science Advisory Committee to the Office of Defense Mobilization, "remarked spontaneously that from the committee's point of view, most matters of policy coming before the president have a very strong scientific component. Not only a technical but a scientific point of view plays a role. He did not see around the president any person who would help keep the president aware of the scientific considerations, as in the economic field. He did not see the scientific point of view put forward in a way to give daily opportunities to influence attitudes. He observed that science was, in a sense, being called in after the fact. There was no continuous involvement. The president said that he agreed with this, and that more than once he had felt this need. But the lines of organization were frozen. The office of the

many reasons, far too many to discuss here,* President Nixon's Reorganization Plan No. 1 of 1973 abolished the Office of Science and Technology, together with PSAC and the Office of Special Assistant. The main point that I wish to make here is not that President Nixon thought he could dispense with science advice, nor that Secretary of State Kissinger had built up a group of personal scientific and technical advisers apart from PSAC, nor even that under the Nixon administration "the White House scientific advisory apparatus had become more of a facade than a reality."† Rather, I believe it to be the case that the need for a presidential scientific apparatus is as great as ever, even though it does not now exist. The easy dismantling of that apparatus, and its nonreplacement for three years, may show what lack of strength the scientific community has in the presidential establishment and in the formation of national policy.‡

The official or public decline of the influence of science in the White House and, to some degree, in the Congress, has been paral-

---

president was crammed and inadequate. Congress has traditionally been jealous with respect to this office. However, something could probably be worked out. It is not the entire answer, but it would help to have someone who could see the scientific problems and bring in more specific ideas — a special assistant trained as a scientist. Dr. Rabi felt the president should have a person with whom he could live easily. The president asked General Goodpaster to mull this over. Dr. Killian pointed out that a committee such as the science advisory committee could provide proper backup for such an individual. The committee could be given recognition and status so the individual would not be isolated from the scientific community. The president said that he had felt a need for such assistance time and again . . ." (Quoted from the informal notes made on that occasion by David Z. Beckler).

  * Among the reasons for the decline and fall of the presidential scientific advisory apparatus, there must be included the general disaffection of the intellectual community (including the scientists as a potent force) during the Nixon administration. On questions such as the ABM and the SST, the members of PSAC would have appeared to have taken on an adversary role to the president, and a public one at that, rather than serving as his confidential friendly advisers. It can also be argued that this confidentiality had been doomed by the Freedom of Information Act.

  † A remark attributed to "a former special assistant to President Kennedy." In fact, the decisions and opinions of PSAC were apparently used by the president only when it was to his political advantage to do so.

  ‡ In January, 1973, Dr. H. Guyford Steever, the Director of NSF, was designated as the president's scientific adviser, but plainly this role is not comparable to that of the special assistant — especially with regard to direct and intimate and regular contact with the president. The Congress, in the meanwhile, has established an Office of Technology Assessment, directed by former Congressman Emilio Q. Daddario, who had won the respect of the scientific community for his general knowledge and understanding of scientific

leled by a loss of faith in science as a universal solver of problems. There seems to me to be little doubt that the current disillusionment with science is a by-product of the exaggerated hopes attached to science only a few years ago, amounting literally to the fallacy of scientism. But, whatever the cause, the faith and confidence in science of an earlier day have been replaced, more and more, by accusations of guilt and complicity: guilt for being responsible for the industrial destruction of the landscape and the increasing pollution of our natural environment, complicity in such war-related crimes as the production of atom bombs and chemicals for the defoliation of Vietnam. A Harris poll of a few years ago showed that although 89 percent of the people interviewed were convinced that "America could never have achieved its high standard of living without scientific progress," and although 81 percent still believed that without "a strong scientific effort, the United States would become a second-rate power," 62 percent of the sample interviewed were convinced that "scientists have thought too much about what will work and not enough about how their discoveries will affect the lives of people." And more than seven out of every ten agreed that science has "gone far beyond our progress in managing our human problems," while an equal number held that one result of science has been that "people don't know what nature is anymore."

In any discussion of science and the American republic, a distinction must be made between science as a system of rationality and values and science as a provider of a better life. That science has been a fecund source of agricultural, medical and technological innovations is undeniable. But the problem of recent years has been the realization that the price to be paid for such innovations or improvements in the material aspects of life may be more than we wanted to pay. In any revaluation of science as a factor in Ameri-

---

matters during his chairmanship of the Sub-Committee for Science, Research and Development of the House Committee for Science and Astronautics. At present writing there are several plans or proposals to establish more effective science advising to the Congress and to reestablish a post of science adviser within the White House. But the fact will always remain that the advising link between the president and the scientific community was so weak and tenuous that, under the Nixon administration, it could be terminated with the ease of switching off the electric light in a White House office. In the concluding volume of the OECD review of *The Research System* (Canada, United States, General Conclusions, vol. 3, 1974), the change that occurred in the Nixon administration is aptly entitled "The Honeymoon Is Over."

can life, we must go beyond the practical problems of food supply, new synthetic substances, means of curing diseases and preserving health, and new modes of manufacturing, making warfare, and providing communication and transportation. Does (or can) science offer the community of man any values that may be significant for his social and political values, his moral and religious tenets, or his spiritual or intellectual life? Or is science merely a source of innovations in the practical sphere that depends on a system of inquiry of fairly recent origin that has been exceptionally successful in gaining knowledge and control of the external environment? The disaffection with science has taken a number of forms, some of which are related to the progress of science itself. In years past, it was believed that the primary characteristic of science was its method, a set of codified rules and procedures which all scientists shared and used and which nonscientists did not. Presumably, in that best of all possible worlds, all actions and decisions—in the political, social, and moral spheres—would be guided by this scientific method.

But today scientists generally agree that there is no such simply codifiable method, even though they may not all go as far as P.W. Bridgman in saying that the vaunted scientific method is nothing else but "doing one's damnedest with one's mind, no holds barred." There has been a tremendous improvement in the science education in secondary schools and colleges, but I fear that this has proved important chiefly for would-be scientists (and doctors and engineers), rather than for the nonscientist citizen. It is a sobering thought that a hundred years ago all college students were expected to devote about a quarter of their course work to science (including a good dose of mathematics), whereas today—in an age of science— that requirement has been watered down to a single course, and that one usually of the "general education" variety. This general ignorance of science is said to be connected with the current complexities of science which transcend the comprehension not only of laymen but even of scientists in neighboring fields. At the same time there is a growing influence of those who demand that science either be abandoned or so modified that it shall cease to be the science we have known. Among the strident voices arguing for such an end to science as we have known it (or the technology now associated in the popular mind with science to a degree that makes the two seem inseparable) are Jacques Ellul, Theodore Roszak, Charles

Reich, and others. It has been proclaimed that "Christian ethics and virtue died as our scientific and technological age was born."* A report prepared at the request of Senator Jackson by the Congressional Research Services noted that the new trend in American culture "implies throwing out the scientific method, the definition of effects, and the search for cause . . . through the processes of rational analysis." This is a far cry, indeed, from Isaac Newton's pious hope, expressed at the conclusion of his *Opticks:*

> And if natural Philosophy in all its Parts, by pursuing this Method, shall at length be perfected, the Bounds of Moral Philosophy will also be enlarged. For so far as we can know by natural Philosophy what is the first Cause, what Powers he has over us, and what Benefits we receive from him, so far our Duty towards him, as well as towards one another, will appear to us in the Light of Nature.

As I contemplate these issues from the point of view of a historian, it seems to me that the current debates often exhibit a confusion of values and judgments. In the eighteenth century—the Age of Reason and of the Enlightenment—it seemed to men of good will that the sciences (especially Newtonian science) offered not only a sound explanation of the functioning of our universe, but provided a model to man for the construction of a similar kind of God-inspired rational order in government and in society. A typical expression of this point of view was given in an allegorical poem by J. T. Desaguliers, one of Newton's chief disciples. It was called *The Newtonian System of the World, the Best Model of Government,* and it was said to contain "a plain and intelligible Account of the System of the World, by Way of *Annotations.*" Since science, through its prophet Isaac Newton, had shown the principles that could be the basis of a better world order, clearly all that was needed was a system of mass education in order to insure that these principles would be generally learned and put to use in the social and political sphere.

Today's critics of science would discard such a model altogether for a number of reasons, among them the admitted fact that this approach to a better world has proved to be too simple, to say nothing of the fact that Newtonian science has grown to become the

---

* This comes from a report in the New York *Times,* 13 June 1973 (quoted by Don K. Price), of an address made by the "recently reelected head of the Southern Baptist Church, himself the retiring president of a chemical corporation."

Frankenstein producing such real and potential monsters as "the bomb," the "genetically synthesized android," the "behavioral brain washer," and the "despot computer."* But there are three main lines of historical argument that such discussion tends to neglect. First, any mature nonutopian scientist or social scientist is fully aware that a sound analysis of society and prescription for its amelioration may make use of the models, concepts, and techniques of the physical and biological sciences, but that this is but a small part of the total intellectual activity in the social-science area. Consequently, we do not any longer (most of us, that is) believe in either the infallibility of physical and biological scientists outside their areas of specialty, nor do we even hope that the social sciences will ever have the degree of unity and simplicity (such as it is) found in the physical and biological sciences. Second, while the scientific utopians (and all those who were seduced by the fallacy of scientism) did believe that science might indeed replace the traditional value-system of ordinary religion, and ultimately produce a religion of nature, they were always few in numbers and their influence has been greatly exaggerated. Science, despite such hopes as Newton's, has never provided an ethical, moral, or social set of values to replace (or to be in conflict with) the traditional values. Third, with the passage of simple utopian hopes and ideals, there should now be a mature rather than a simpleminded approach to this dual scientific enterprise—at once an assault on the unknown and a source of new technology, agriculture, and medicine. Of course, uncontrolled technology—whether science-based or not—is always, and cannot help but be, a source of potential and actual danger to our lives and our environment. But one does not give up the use of fire for cooking our food and heating our homes because fire destroys the forests and may burn up our houses and our factories.

It seems to me, as I look at the major problems that the world faces today (and here I leave my role as historian), that we do not need less science, but more science. For mankind as a whole has to face the basic challenges of a population that is already growing to the limits of the traditional boundaries for the normal support of life. Even more important than the provision of the material necessities (clothing, shelter, tools, medicines) are those twin world requirements of food and available energy. The advance of the

---

* These are the "monsters" referred to in a recent article by Theodore Roszak.

size of the population will not be stopped, except possibly by a holo-
caust too horrible to imagine; how will we even attempt to increase
the food production and energy supply of the world if we do not
do it through science? To turn away from science today is, in my
opinion, a selfish and morally disgraceful act that is in essence to
turn our backs on the needs of the future and coming generations of
our fellowmen. Honest analysis shows that the unbridled power of a
science-based technology carries with it extreme dangers to man
and to society, and that some aspects of scientific research may open
up ever-new sources of potential danger. But I hope that man shall
be able to rise to such challenges, no longer expecting science to
be the font of only beneficent gifts, but aware—at last—of the
problems and complexities for good or evil in all of man's creations,
including science and technology. Perhaps the test of this nation
shall be, in the years to come, whether or not we were capable of
developing and using our science in such ways as to assure the
maximum benefits of its applications for all men, while still intelligently controlling and regulating the uses to which such science is
put, thus keeping to a minimum the deleterious, harmful, and unde-
sired consequences.

Such a process would require a synergistic effort by scientists,
engineers, social scientists and statesmen—on a level and to a degree
that the world has not hitherto known. Am I myself being now as
chiliastic as those nineteenth-century utopians whom I have charged
with having embraced the fallacy of scientism? I hope not. For I
see before us the beginnings of just such an attitude of responsibility.
In times past, when scientists produced a new antibiotic, it was
generally considered that that job was done: one more disease conquered! But now all scientists are aware of the need to be alert for
(and to try to find) the possible side effects that may mitigate the
benefits of the cure. In at least one case (recombinant DNA), the
scientists themselves have been so alert to the potential or imagined
dangers that they have set up their own regulations concerning
possible allowable kinds of experiments. Scientists and engineers developed principles and practice that made it possible to build and
fly a supersonic transport; but their job did not end there. These
scientists and engineers then raised their voices to demand the exploration of the possible or potential deleterious effects such SST's
might have on the environment and on the quality of life. And so
I believe that we have beginnings, however small, of the ways in

which mankind may develop in the future a saner and more beneficial control of his own inventiveness: a control based on reason, experience, and innate and accumulated wisdom.

The middle portion of this article is to some degree based on an earlier publication, *Science and American Society in the First Century of the Republic*.

In Praise of Particularity: The Concept of Mediating Structures

Peter L. Berger

From the beginning the American republic conceived of itself as
a great experiment in the realization of liberty. This experiment
has come to be conjoined, serendipitously, with another fact about
America—its peculiar relationship to the process of modernization.
Talcott Parsons has called America "the lead society." This is not
an expression of nationalist megalomania, but rather a descriptive
(if you will, a "value-free") statement to the effect that a number
of modernizing forces have gone further in this country than anywhere else. It is in this double sense that I am prepared to use the
term *chosen* for America. For better or for worse, we are the most
modernized society in the contemporary world. And, audaciously,
we continue to carry on the experiment of free institutions in this
not necessarily enviable condition. Liberty is on the retreat today
all over the world. I cannot pursue here the far-reaching, and
sinister, implications of this for America's role on the international
scene. But the institutions that embody liberty are also under great
pressure domestically. My observations in what follows pertain to
this domestic crisis. They are animated by the hope that, if we can
resolve this crisis without abandoning the experiment, we may still
serve as a lesson for the human race. Perhaps we are "chosen" to
do this.

The following remarks are concerned with an attempt to link
sociological theory and public policy. There is something vaguely
disreputable even about saying this. Sociologists are supposed to
come in two kinds. There is the larger group, which consists of
people intimately related to computers and other mathematical
gadgets; these people make costly studies of very specific areas of
social life; they report on these studies in barbaric English; once in
a while, their findings have a bearing on this or that issue of public
policy. Then there is a smaller group, consisting of people who are
all in sociology by some sort of biographical mistake (they really
should be in philosophy or literature); these people mostly write
books about the theories of dead Germans; as far as public policy is
concerned, this theorizing has no relevance at all—and a good thing

it is. Broadly speaking, this was the generally perceived division of
the species "sociologist" when I was a student in the 1950's; after a
short interlude, this seems to be the general perception once more.
For a brief period, in the late 1960's, this dichotomy was challenged: sociological theory was called on to be politically relevant.
Of those who responded to this clarion call, there are few left today;
most of them have simply switched their allegiance from one set of
dead Germans to another set of even deader ones; the rest, with
some relief, have returned to the comforting mysteries of quantita-
tive techniques.

Occasionally I get the feeling that I'm the last convert to the
message that sociological theorists should become politically
relevant. (Lest this remark be misinterpreted as betraying delusions
of grandeur, let me hasten to add that this feeling is one of pure
paranoia.) Like many others, I was sucked into political relevance
by my opposition to the Vietnam war, which turned my attention—
first political, only later social-scientific—to the Third World. In
consequence, for several years the focus of my work was problems
of modernization and development; and while some of this work
was quite theoretical, it was not possible (nor did I want it to be
possible) to divorce the theoretical problems from the urgent
political questions. Actually, I was surprised myself when I discovered that my sociological theorizing was, in places, very relevant
indeed to questions of development policy. I did not follow the
much-traveled route from this discovery into Marxist scholasticism.
Neither did I, at this late stage, transform myself into the kind of
person who can talk to a computer. What I did do was to turn my
attention back to this country: if sociological theory can be relevant
to public policy in Third World countries, who knows, it may have
a comparable relevance in America.

Let me be a little more specific now. One funny thing that happened to me in the Third World was that I developed a strong
sympathy with tribalism. This was all the more surprising as it was
contrary to my own values as well as my own biography—I have
always been deracinated, cosmopolitan, and totally unattracted to
what Marx so aptly called the idiocy of village life. But, while I
have no desire personally to find some all-embracing *Gemeinschaft*
as a refuge from the rootlessness of modernity, I gained an enormous respect for the positive human values of such intact premodern communities as still exist in the Third World: communities

of kinship, tribe, locality and region, and the frequently moving efforts to preserve these communities under the violent pressures of modernization. Conversely, I gained a better understanding of the price exacted by modernity. I have no wish to romanticize tribalism. Rather, I think that an appreciation of the human significance of tribalism (taking that term in its broadest possible sense) can be of great help in *a critique of modernity* (and please note that a critique is *not* an attack, *not* a blanket rejection). Such a critique spans the theoretical and the political levels. My present work on mediating structures comes out of these concerns (at the moment I'm engaged in elaborating the public-policy implications of the basic concept, in collaboration with Richard Neuhaus, in a project funded by the American Enterprise Institute).

What are mediating structures? The concept has quite vast implications, but it can be defined simply: mediating structures are those institutions which stand between the individual in his private sphere and the large institutions of the public sphere. The concept is by no means new; indeed, a good case can be made that it is a central theme of the sociological tradition. What might be new, however, is the translation of the concept into a paradigm for public policy, in the very specific conditions of American politics today. A *locus classicus* of the concept is on the last pages of Emile Durkheim's *Suicide,* where he describes the "tempest" of modernization, sweeping away what he calls the "little aggregations" in which people existed through most of human history, leaving only the state on the one hand and a mass of individuals, "like so many liquid molecules," on the other hand. Very similar analyses can be found in the classical German sociologists (Ferdinand Tönnies, Max Weber, Georg Simmel), and in this country in the works of Charles Cooley, Thorstein Veblen and the writers of the Chicago School. Talcott Parsons and Robert Nisbet have made important contributions to this conceptualization in recent American sociology. If one wants to pursue the concept beyond the sociological tradition, one may go back to earlier sources, which very interestingly are both on the Right and the Left of the political-ideological spectrum. One may refer to Edmund Burke (insisting on the importance of "small platoons" as the foundation for all wider loyalties), Alexis de Tocqueville (finding in voluntary associations one of the keys to the vitality of American democracy), and Otto von Gierke (with his fixation on the alleged virtues of medieval guilds). At the same time, one may refer to sources on the Left, within Marxism, and even more clearly in the anarcho-syndicalist tradition. But it is not my intention here to give a history-of-ideas treatment. Instead, let me explicate the concept, necessarily in very brief form, as I understand it in my own sociological theorizing.

Modernization brings about a novel dichotomization of social life. The dichotomy is between the huge and immensely powerful institutions of the public sphere (the state, the large economic agglomerates that we now know as corporations and labor unions, and the ever-growing bureaucracies that administer sectors of society not properly political or economic, such as education or the organized professions) and the private sphere, which is a curious interstitial area "left over," as it were, by the large institutions and indeed (in the words of Arnold Gehlen) marked by "underinstitutionalization." Put more simply, the dichotomy is between the megastructures and private life. These two spheres of modern society are experienced by the individual in very different ways. The megastructures are remote, often hard to understand or downright unreal, impersonal, and ipso facto unsatisfactory as sources for individual meaning and identity. In the classical Marxian term, the megastructures are "alienating." By contrast, private life is experienced as the single most important area for the discovery and the actualization of meaning and identity. While, of course, the megastructures impose limits and controls on private life, they also leave the individual (at least in Western societies) a remarkable degree of freedom in shaping his private life. The latter is underinstitutionalized in the precise degree to which the individual is left to his own devices in a wide range of activities that are crucial to the formation of a meaningful identity, from expressing his religious preference to settling on a sexual life-style. This is heady stuff. It is also asking a lot of the individual; in effect, it is asking him to create his own private world *de novo,* with few and unreliable institutional supports in this audacious assignment. In the well-known Durkheimian term, private life is always under the shadow of *anomie.* Modernization therefore breeds alienation and anomie, which is another way of saying that modernity has a built-in crisis which, once set in motion, is very difficult to resolve.

As long as the individual can indeed find meaning and identity in his private life, he can manage to put up with the meaningless and disidentifying world of the megastructures. For many people the formula for this adjustment goes something like this: "I put in my time on the job between 9 and 5, I pay my taxes, I don't upset any applecarts in my union—and then I go home, where I can really be myself." In other words, as long as private life is *not* anomic, the alienations of the megastructures are at least tolerable. The situation becomes intolerable if "home," that refuge of stability and value in an alien world, ceases to be such a refuge—when, say, my wife leaves me, my children take on life-styles that are strange and unacceptable to me, my church becomes incomprehensible, my neighborhood becomes a place of danger, and so forth. The very underinstitutionalization of private life, however, makes it quite likely that my home will indeed be threatened by these or similar anomic disintegrations. Conversely, the best defenses against the threat are those institutions, however weakened, which still give a measure of stability to private life. These are, precisely, the mediating institutions, notably those of family, church, voluntary association, neighborhood and subculture.

The mediating structures, then, are essential if private life is to remain "home." This does not mean that they have to continue in their traditional forms. It is quite possible that there may be new forms of family, church or subculture, and that these may become the institutional anchorage for individual meaning and identity, always provided that they acquire the necessary degree of stability, that they can be relied upon. It is equally important to see that the mediating structures are *also* essential for the megastructures, and especially for those that constitute the political order in a modern society. Why? The reasons are actually quite simple: no society, modern or otherwise, can survive without what Durkheim called a "collective conscience," that is, without moral values that have general authority. The megastructures, because of their remoteness and sheer vastness, are very unsuitable for the generation and maintenance of such a general morality. Bureaucrats are the poorest of *moralistes*. The megastructures, and especially the state, must depend for, let us say, "moral sustenance" on institutions or social formations that are "below" them. They must do so, to be exact, unless coercion is to replace moral authority as the basis of political order. But neither can a general morality rest upon the unstable and unreliable efforts of atomized individuals engaged in private experiments of "life-styling." The social contract cannot be renegotiated every day by millions of individual "consenting adults," not unless society is to lapse into intermittent chaos. To be sure, there are ways in which the megastructures, especially the political ones, can modify their own institutional organization so as to be less remote, less alienating, by the various modalities of democratic accountability, openness to grass-roots initiatives, by decentralization or debureaucratization. Such modifications are, indeed, recurring goals of the democratic ideal. It is very unlikely, all the same, that these modifications will ever be adequate substitutes for those structures that mediate between the political order and the home life of individuals, and if they became such substitutes, the democratic ideal, certainly in its American version, would be in great trouble.

Let me sum up the argument thus far. The progressive disintegration of mediating structures constitutes a double crisis. It is a crisis on the level of individual life. It is also a political crisis. Without mediating structures, private life comes to be engulfed in a deepening anomie. Without mediating structures, the political order is drawn into the same anomie by being deprived of the moral foundation upon which it rests. Since the political order, unlike the individual, cannot commit suicide or go insane (though it might be argued that there are political analogues to suicide and insanity), it is confronted with the necessity of substituting coercion for moral consent. One does not have to be a sociological theorist to perceive that this substitution has, if nothing else, the one great virtue of simplification. It seems to me that just this is a major psychological clue to the otherwise incomprehensible attraction of totalitarian movements and regimes: totalitarianism promises to resolve the dichotomy of private and public; it keeps the promise in a perverse way, by so politicizing the private that it is absorbed in the public.

This is not the place to pursue these questions of political psychology. But I want to turn to a different if related question. How do the major political ideologies relate to mediating structures?

The broad tradition of liberal ideology, all the way back to the Enlightenment, has an especially close relationship to the process of modernization. Indeed, the argument can be made that this tradition embodies the myth of modernity more than any other. It is not surprising, then, that it has been singularly blind to the importance and at times even the very existence of mediating structures. Liberalism is, above all, a faith in rationality. Its designs for society are highly rational, abstract, universalistic. Burke, in criticizing the programs of the French revolutionaries, aptly called them "geometrical." Liberalism, of course, has undergone profound transformations since then, in France as elsewhere. In America, as has often been pointed out, liberalism underwent a remarkable conversion in this century, basically a conversion from faith in the market to faith in government (paradoxically, those adhering to the older version of the liberal creed now call themselves conservatives). Yet the underlying faith in the powers of rationality has remained unchanged. While before the anonymous forces of the market (Adam Smith's "invisible hand") were supposed to make human affairs come out in accord with rationality, now the planning and controls of government are expected to achieve that salvific result. It is precisely the mediating structures that stand in the way of this "geometry." They are "irrational" (that is, based on emotion and value, not on functional utility), concrete, highly particularistic, and ipso facto resistant to the rationales of either market or government. In terms of contemporary American liberalism, the sundry "irrationalities" of human life are firmly assigned to the private sphere (where liberals are indeed sincerely committed to protecting them under the rubric of individual rights). As far as public policy is concerned, "geometry" continues to reign. No better up-to-date illustration of this can be found than the liberally inspired designs for racial integration in places like Boston or Louisville; abstract "geometries" imposed without regard for the fabric of communities in which people live their daily lives. These designs bear an uncomfortable resemblance to those concocted by liberal social scientists engaged in "nation building" in Vietnam. Those too were abstract "geometries" with no relation to the living fabric of society—and, significantly, there was the same mania for quantification.

The Left tradition of political ideology (which, *in nuce,* is the tradition of socialist thought) has been more clear-sighted in this matter. It is no accident that alienation occupies the place it does in Marxist thought. I would indeed contend that the protest against the abstractions of modernity is at the heart of the socialist ideal: socialism is a faith in renewed community. The weakness of the Left perception is that it ascribes alienation to capitalism alone and thus fails to see that the abolition of capitalism brings on new alienations of even greater potency, namely, the alienations of the socialist state, a political formation that (at any rate to date) has shown itself to be endemically totalitarian. The contemporary American Left fully shares this weakness. It perceives the alienating power of those megastructures that are linked to capitalism (the currently favorite target, of course, is the multinational corporation); it is totally blind to the realities of the socialist regimes it admires (usually these are varieties of oriental despotism masquerading as Marxist); in its disdain for the irrationalities of mediating structures (family, church, and so on), it stands squarely in the liberal tradition of the Enlightenment. The New Left of the mid-1960's, especially in its linkages with the anarcho-syndicalist elements of the counterculture, showed some promise of overcoming this weakness. In all likelihood, this kind of New Left thinking is now a matter of the past.

Classical European conservatism, as exemplified by Burke, was vibrantly aware of the importance of mediating structures. *Its* weakness was an inability to perceive the irreversible realities of modernization, a clinging to premodern imagery, and in consequence an inability to generate viable policies for a modern society. As far as contemporary America is concerned, this classical conservatism has little if any relevance (*pace* the ritual invocations of Burke's name in places like *National Review*). Contemporary American conservatism is Old Testament liberalism. Its quarrel with the latter-day liberal covenant of the New Deal is interesting, even important, but of little help with regard to the point at issue. Contemporary American conservatives do indeed perceive the alienations of big government; they are quite blind to the alienations of big business; their faith in the allegedly benign rationality of market forces is a wonder to behold. Even so, it must be said in fairness that it is in these circles, along with the circles of what remains of the New Left and the counterculture, that one finds some measure of understanding of mediating structures.

This rapid survey of the ideological spectrum thus leads to a negative result: nowhere on this spectrum is the concept of mediating structures really at home. But a positive conclusion may be drawn from this. Precisely for this reason is the concept politically promising. *It cuts across the ideological divides.* At a moment of history when many people, in all the different political camps, feel that the old ideologies have become sterile and that new starting points are needed, this cutting-across quality of the concept of mediating structures makes it politically interesting. This becomes clear, I think, as one passes from general considerations to concrete policy implications. One finds then that these implications jump back and forth between conventionally right-wing and left-wing positions. In other words, the concept slices reality up in new ways.

In the project I'm working on with Richard Neuhaus, we have formulated two overall policy propositions, both based on the understanding outlined above of the importance of mediating institutions in society. One: *Public policy should protect and foster mediating structures.* Two: *Wherever possible, public policy should utilize the mediating structures as its agents.* The two propositions could be called, respectively, minimalist and maximalist. Minimally, the message to government is: leave these institutions alone! Maximally, the message is: see where you can actually use these institutions. The two, of course, are not necessarily contradictory. One may apply to some policy areas, the other to different areas. On the whole, the minimal injunction is more palatable to those on the Right, the maximal one to those farther Left (one could put this observation cynically by saying that, with appropriate modifications, the concept could be written into either the Republican or the Democratic platform), though this bifurcation does not always hold.

The empirical presupposition of the minimalist proposition is that many programs of public policy have actively hurt mediating structures, to the great detriment of the society. The remedy is that public policy should cease and desist. This injunction in itself represents an amplification of the liberal value of civil liberties and rights. It suggests that the protections of the latter should extend to certain communities and communal institutions as well as to individuals.

A few concrete examples: public policy should desist from forcing welfare mothers to go to work and turn their children over to day-care centers. This, of course, is but a particularly obnoxious aspect of much broader welfare policies that have been detrimental to family stability among the poor, a point that has been amply documented, especially for the black community. Public policy, and especially the courts, should reverse the recent interpretation of the First Amendment as signifying the legal establishment of a secularist creed at the expense of the historic religious traditions of the society. The Supreme Court decision on prayer in the public schools was a high point of this secularist wave, but by no means an end point. There is now a case in the courts of New York that challenges the right of religious social-work agencies to employ religious criteria in assigning children for adoption; if resolved in favor of the plaintiffs, the case would result in a massive assault on the liberty and integrity of religious communities. Largely under the heading of fighting corruption and/or inefficiency, public policy tends to favor public social-work agencies over private ones. Alliances of professional organizations and government agencies impose standards on private agencies that, very often, have no real function other than driving these agencies out of business. This is but part of a general animus against voluntary associations, be they working in welfare, health or education. Our proposition is that voluntarism should be encouraged, not hampered, by public policy. Mention has already been made of the assault on neighborhoods in the name of racial integration. Of course racial justice should be very high on the agenda of public policy in this country. There are many ways in which public policy can promote this goal, not only by proscriptive legislation but through positive programs (especially in employment, housing and education); many of these programs, in all likelihood, will have little relation to mediating structures. But the current court-enforced bussing programs are, almost without exception, an exercise in profound sociological folly. Unless reversed, these policies will have severely detrimental effects on urban life (including the goal of racial justice). Public policy, especially in the area of education, has tended to be indifferent if not hostile to the racial, ethnic and religious diversity of American society. The black movement has been first in sharply challenging this leveling (and ipso facto anomie-generating) tendency. The same challenge has now been taken up by Hispanics, American Indians and various groups involved in the revival of white ethnicity. No doubt there are dangers in this (including the danger of cultural and political Balkanization recurrently brought up by liberal critics). Nevertheless there is good reason to welcome this new awareness of the vital role of subcultures in the, let us say, moral constitution of this country. Without abandoning the rights of the individual apart from any subculture, public policy should protect, not seek to destroy, the living subcultures from which people derive meaning and identity. Bilingualism in education is one interesting issue in this context.

The maximalist proposition, needless to say, is the much riskier one. The biggest risk was well put by one critic of our project, when he suggested that one of the worst things that could happen was great government enthusiasm for this proposition. Eventually there might even be a Secretary for Mediating Structures in the cabinet—and that might well be the end of mediating structures. Agents of public policy are subject to public controls. Are there ways of having public policy utilize mediating structures without destroying them in the process? I have no definitely reassuring answer to this question, and it troubles me. Still, I think that there are possibilities to be explored here.

Probably the most auspicious model for the maximalist proposition is the voucher concept in education. Various versions of this concept have been discussed, and there is now going on some very modest experimentation along its lines. It is a model for the following reasons. It does not represent a retreat from public involvement in this particular area of social life; it only represents a retreat from one exclusive modality through which public involvement has hitherto been expressed. It empowers people to make decisions who have no decision-making power in this area now (more specifically, it gives lower-income families the power to make the same decisions on the education of their children that higher-income families have already). It respects the pluralism of American life. It may also be, alas, a model for the furious opposition it has aroused from an odd alliance of vested interests: the bureaucratic establishment of public education and the teachers' unions, both of whom have an interest (in the case of the unions, possibly, a perceived rather than a real one) in maintaining the status quo of educational monopoly, liberals worried about cultural Balkanization, and militant secularists opposed to any form of public support of religious institutions. The voucher concept, as applied to education, touches on every one of the mediating structures enumerated: family, church, voluntary association, neighborhood and subculture. For this reason, one of the questions we are thinking about is how in other areas of public policy, besides education, analogues to the voucher concept might be designed. But this is not the only direction along which one may think in exploring the maximalist proposition. Some other examples go like this. The concepts of family income maintenance and/or children's allowances. Tax incentives for voluntary efforts (religiously sponsored as well as other) in attacking various social problems. Decentralization and community control of some functions of municipal government (including law enforcement and health delivery). Zoning and housing policies that work with rather than against existing communities and/or life-styles (always with the proviso that such policies are not racially exclusive and do not infringe on the rights of individuals).

To list these examples is to acknowledge the immense complexity of these issues of public policy. I am well aware of this. The concept of mediating structures is no panacea, but rather the starting point for very careful, prudent explorations. Yet it was necessary here to become very concrete, in order to show the direct line that goes from very broad considerations of sociological theory to the highly specific problems that occupy people in the day-by-day business of public policy.

Let me come to the close. The history of freedom in the modern world has for a long time been marked by the often conflicting claims of universalism and particularity. The main thrust of modernity has always been universalizing, and nothing in the foregoing seeks to deny the liberating effects of this universalism for countless human beings. However, as with most human endeavors, universalism pushed to an extreme becomes destructive. The "liquid molecules" of individuals caught in a chaotic private world on the one hand, and the leveling tyranny of the totalitarian state on the other hand, these are the twin consequences of universalism gone berserk. It is time, I believe, to return to a praise of particularity. It is especially time for this in America. The prospects for freedom, and indeed for anything that could be called political decency, are very dim on the contemporary scene. Our time continues to be viewed by some as an age of liberation; it increasingly appears, in fact, as an age of spreading oppression and deepening misery. America is one of the very few places left in which there is at least a fighting chance for innovations and experiments within the framework of free institutions. There is also a specifically American tradition of balancing universalism and particularity, of pluralism, of combining the power of the modern state with the energies of voluntary associations. The concept of mediating structures, as applied to public policy in this country, may be one way of revitalizing an American political heritage that seems all the more precious as, every day, it seems more in peril.

Is America in Any Sense Chosen?
A Black Response
Vincent Harding

Let me begin with a statement of my own ambivalence in this setting—and of my struggle to overcome it. As many of you must surely know, there are large numbers of blacks and other nonwhites who continue to have profound misgivings about any level of participation in the current American parade of bicentennial events. And I share many of the feelings of that group. We do not celebrate, cannot celebrate, what most of white America celebrates.

To celebrate the birth of this nation would be to glorify the bondage of our foreparents, for it was the founders of this "new nation" who enslaved us; it was the original Constitution of this grand experiment which guaranteed our slavery. That, of course, was only the beginning of our sorrows. So, were we to enter the mainstream of the self-promoting line of bicentennial marchers, we would need to become amnesiacs to the most cruel elements of our own history in this land. It would require that we become deaf to the different drums of our forebears, that we blind ourselves to the rivers of blood through which we have had to fight on our way to this limited stage of freedom.

Considering this necessary black opposition to much that passes for bicentennial business in America, I was encouraged to read in the conference statement those words:

> Many bicentennial celebrations will examine the drama of outer history in America. Notre Dame and St. Mary's have chosen to direct themselves . . . to the drama of inner history, which is the story of failed vision as well as noble vision, of virtue realized and unrealized.

Even though the statement ends with an evocation of Lincoln's "almost chosen people," and even though I am very well aware that he did not include my people in that chosen company, I still take the search for our inner history as a point of engagement with this conference, and I have come, hesitant, but with a sense of necessity.

I say necessity because I think that I *must* participate, and must

119

unofficially represent in this drama that deepest, darkly burning core of America's history, which is the story of its nonwhite peoples. Looking from their perspective, I must speak more of their hope and of the failure of others. But I must speak, for ultimately I am convinced that we who come from the inner depths of the nation's history, who represent both the brokenness and the dream, who have fought our way to this stage, are now also morally obliged to engage in the most active struggles of the next period of American history. And I am convinced that these will no longer simply be struggles to be heard, to be noticed, to be treated equally, justly, to be allowed into America. All those conflicts, though terribly incomplete, must now remain as broken arrows of truth as we press on to engage in the harder, harsher, more excellent struggle for a fundamental redefining and reshaping of the American nation itself.

In such a setting, the struggle for intellectual and spiritual redefinitions is an essential point of grounding, and I seek to participate in that arena now. So, from out of the center of our hidden history, I wish to move directly to address the question: "Is America in Any Sense Chosen?"

My search for a response to that question has been at once mediated and stimulated by two literary texts from the nonwhite worlds of the Americas. The first represents only a snatch of conversation from Carlos Fuentes' important Mexican novel, *Where the Air Is Clear*. Near the beginning of the work, two of Fuentes' characters are discussing the question of the search for their own personal origins, and the origins of their society (in a certain sense, asking about chosenness, I think). While one man speaks of the necessity of tracing his bloodline back into history to seek out origins, the second person, representing Fuentes, disagrees and says, "Rather than born original, we come to be original; origin is creation. Mexico must find her origin by looking ahead, not behind . . . we have to create our beginning and our originality."

I confess that I am not always fully certain about the most precise meanings of Fuentes' fascinating words, but I am urgently drawn into their presence by implications which I catch, by a sense of cords which tie the future to the past, cords which gather and take their power from the hard choices and moral struggles of the present. Whatever their fullest meanings, the words of the Mexican writer are surely akin to the sentiments expressed by Langston Hughes in one of his best-known poems of the 1930's:

O, let America be America again—
The land that never has been yet—
And yet must be—
The land where *every* man is free.
The land that's mine—
The poor man's, Indian's, Negro's, ME—
Who made America,
Whose sweat and blood, whose faith and pain,
Whose hand at the foundry, whose plow in the rain,
Must bring back our mighty dream again.

. . . . . .

O, yes,
I say it plain,
America never was America to me,
And yet I swear this oath—
America will be!
An ever-living seed,
Its dream
Lies deep in the heart of me.

We, the people, must redeem
Our land, the mines, the plants, the rivers,
The mountains and the endless plain—
All, all the stretch of these great green states—
And make America again!*

In a sense, everything that I have to say is really a meditation on history, seen through the prism of these two works; for they strengthen my own burgeoning conviction that men and women, peoples, nations, indeed humankind, may create their own chosenness. What I assume is that humans are forever faced with choices about the future—choices, for instance, regarding the need for new beginnings—and that in their decisions about whether to fight, to seize the future, to create a more truly human way, they determine their chosenness for any given point in the history of the race's development. This ever-present opportunity for critical choice, for new creation, for the molding of origins, for the continuous remaking of societies, is a fundamental assumption of this article. It is basic to my understanding of chosenness—at least for my present purpose.

---

* Langston Hughes, "Let America Be America Again." (*Reprinted* by permission of Harold Ober Associates, Inc. © 1938 by Langston Hughes. Renewed.)

So, remembering errands into the wilderness which decimated the occupants of this land, remembering cities on a hill which finally sent their burning lights smashing into Hiroshima and Nagasaki, remembering manifest destinies which included my slavery and Vietnam's great sorrow, I avoid the idea of chosenness in most of its traditional, American, metaphysical senses of the word. Rather, I seek to emphasize that fundamentally, intrinsically human potential within all of us, each of us, to be creators of our future, choosers of our destiny, and therefore recreators, redeemers of our past.

Such an essentially humanistic understanding of chosenness has its own set of pitfalls, of course, but I grasp it with my eyes open to them. And from its perspective, standing with Teilhard de Chardin, I am also suggesting that all women and men, all human societies, live and have their being within the context of our species' evolution to more human levels of life and creativity. As a result, we are all available to that chosenness which grows out of our decision to become more human, to advance ourselves, to enhance other persons, to advance the race to new levels of community, of capacity, of hope, of service.

America fits into that scheme, as one among the many nations who have the capacity for chosenness. However, to stand on more specific grounds, I think the movements of history, of previous choices, here and elsewhere, good and bad, have all placed this nation since its beginning in a position from which it could make a signal contribution to the central human concerns for community and integrity, for justice and equality, especially where the complex and harrowing issue of race is concerned. Thus it has been possible at various points in our history for this country—especially its white majority—to *come* to be chosen, to decide to move forward in the van of humankind's deepest growth and development.

And it is precisely here that the failure and brokenness of our terribly shared history are obvious. For at almost every point of its development, when faced with the opportunity to move self-consciously and steadfastly towards radical restructuring of the basic white-nonwhite relationships, the white majority nation has chosen not to press on beyond grudging concessions and compromises. Indeed, in those times of political crises, instead of advancing towards the hardest, steepest limits of self-transformation for racial justice, the nation has usually chosen to storm the heights of military-industrial technology, capital accumulation and imperialistic adventures.

Only in the context of such a reading of history can one fully appreciate the meaning of the voices of Fuentes and Hughes as they speak for the nonwhite creators of America's inner history. In the agonies of their voices, they represent the offer of, the call to, the chosenness which humans mediate to one another. Through generations, centuries of attacks, pleadings, petitions and the sheer, amazing act of standing, running endurance, these nonwhite peoples have offered an opportunity to their white counterparts to participate in the creation of a truly new nation. These terribly beautiful voices in the wilderness (and the lives which paid dearly for their beauty) have cried out the need for a new society in America which would press humanity's movement forward towards surprising levels of its own still undiscovered capacity for healing. Indeed, looking at the nonwhite group I know best, I cannot avoid the conclusion that it has been the "moral aspirations" of black people in America—shared by other embattled forces—which have created much of the inner history of this country, much of the best vision, much of the hope, only to have it repeatedly smashed by the "moral aspirations" of white America.

I trust that the evidence for such statements needs only the most summary citation. I shall not venture to deal with the native American experience, save to remember the offers which were made by them to the earliest European settlers, offers to share the land and its bounties, to allow for different styles of life to emerge together in one place. And we all know what the response was to that first invitation to chosenness.

Two hundred years ago, when the cries of equality before God and the right of revolution were raised by white revolutionary forces along the Atlantic seaboard and through the scattered inland settlements, blacks offered their own opportunity, put forth an invitation to the revolutionaries to make the truth of their doctrines live on levels yet undreamed by most patriots. Black petitioners, black runaways, black soldiers, black plaintiffs, all called for a truly new nation, one which would not exclude the children of Africa from its best promises. In response, those who were creating America chose to write the institution of black slavery into the nation's constitution. Indeed, under the new government, slavery and the slave trade immediately expanded, eventually making America a slave nation in which only war and rebellion could break the institution. (And from that point on, the literature of black people smashed one of the golden ifs of history: what would America have been if it had seized its chance to be chosen, if it had not built fetters into its very foundations?)

By the end of the Civil War, another chance was available for the remolding of America, based in the conquered Southern territories. Slavery had been destroyed by the horrible power of warfare and the irresistible self-activity of hundreds of thousands of runaway blacks. New institutions, new states, new human relations were seeking for life. Blacks all over the South and throughout the nation lifted their voices and offered their lives for the building of a truly new South, one which would steadily hack away every vestige of slavery and instill new levels of equality and justice in its place. For a brief, fascinating half a decade, this seemed possible. For a glimmering, it appeared as if all the black, resplendent visions would be forced into reality, visions of land, of votes, of forever free children, of education, of jobs, of repayment for unrequited toil, of equal protection and full participation in the building of a new society. And at some points it even seemed possible that there would be realized all the black hopes of a healed and humanized relationship between those who had been the bondsmen and those who had held them down.

But the vision was betrayed and the hope was crushed, for America rejected this new stage in human development. Such chosenness would have required options which would violently wrench the old white supremist and burgeoning capitalist prop out from under the society. Few white Americans were prepared to pay this cost for a truly new nation, for a chosenness of vast significance, for a new encounter with their black inner history. Instead, following the hopes of Lincoln, it was primarily the wounds of whites which were bound up after the war, and the reconciled forces of North and South were then able to return to the ways of unambiguous white supremacy, able to continue the relentless herding and destruction of the natives of the land all over the western territories, were able to build a new Jerusalem of steel and gold and railroad tracks—and go on errands into the wilderness of Hawaii, Cuba and the Philippines.

In spite of many valiant and significant attempts to confront the nation with its own best vocation in the following decades, it was not until the 1950's that the next great movement for national renewal was forced. In the confluence of a vast array of fundamental,

universal challenges to white Western hegemony, America, leader
of the free (white) world, was finally aroused again by its black
inner voice. At that point, the moral aspirations of black America
broke out into a radically new level of confrontation with white
America, offering the entire society another, unparalleled opportunity to proclaim its chosenness, to recreate its destiny and its past.

This time, the call was accompanied by the marching, moving
sounds of hundreds of thousands of feet, mostly black, but with an
episodic white following. This time the call was spread from the
heart of Mississippi to the ghettos of Watts and Roxbury. This time
the invitation to chosenness was presented in songs from the African-
ized Christian tradition and in loud and threatening voices from
the Nation of Islam. It rose out of jails. It burned flashing, fiery
signals high over the skies of Los Angeles, Detroit and Newark, and
hundreds of other cities. It created for a time a new, annealed community of black folk, whose lives had passed through the unifying
beckoning flames.

The call was for freedom, for justice, for equal rights, for equal
access to everything; the call was for jobs, for housing, for land, for
space; the call was for power, for the right to be black, for the destruction of white racism. Sometimes the call was simply for loot.
But at its deepest level, the call was for America to remake itself, to
create its chosenness. Did not the black movement's best-known
prophet speak often of the promise to "redeem the soul of America"?

For a time, especially at the height of the marching feet and the
blazing signals in the skies, a nation seemed to be moving itself, facing itself, admitting what it really had been, all as a prologue to
fundamental transformation, as a movement towards chosenness.
A Southern president quoted from the theme song of the black
movement; a Congress voted new laws; ordinary citizens began to
ask if it might not indeed be time for a new beginning; whites and
blacks began to see each other with new eyes and hear each other
with new ears. Plans were laid for new housing, new jobs, new
black power. People began to speak of radical, fundamental transformation more than at any time since the depression of the 1930's,
to speak of it as if it were possible.

But the response was also ambivalent. For at the same time,
government-sponsored "intelligence" forces were spying, subverting,
provoking, lying, killing. At the same time, private business was
looking for ways to avoid any fundamental change, searching in-

stead for ways to cash in on everything possible, making plans for selling blackness, and thereby corrupting it. At the same time, intransigent hearts and minds were digging in at new battle lines of whiteness, in jobs, in communities, in schools, in spirits. At the same time, a vicious, racist and imperialist war was being fought against another nonwhite people in Vietnam. At the same time, blacks were increasingly divided over the direction and the goals of the next stages of the struggle. And at the same time, men were aiming guns at our leaders and shooting them down. Everywhere: on a street in Jackson, Mississippi, on a stage in Harlem, on a balcony in Memphis, in a bed in Chicago, in a prison yard called Attica. Everywhere. We who chose to be chosen, we who moved out of slavery to call America to freedom, to its own best possible humanity, we paid the price for our chosenness, offering perhaps a sign.

But let us stay with the point, and the point is that in this most recent period of black demands upon the humanity of America, the nation eventually chose to give in to many of its meanest urgings, to take the easy way. It chose in other words to betray again its own initial spasmodic, frightened movements forward towards new black-white life (again, when it betrayed us it betrayed itself, for America cannot be chosen apart from us).

Once the black pressure began to be released it was easy to retreat. And the pressure was released, partly because we blacks lacked the vision and the strength to regroup for the next stages beyond civil rights and symbolic black power, partly because there was no disciplined, revolutionary black leadership to carry the mass movement into its next, higher stage, partly because the counterinsurgency of Operation Chaos and other such elements were too powerful. The pressure was released, partly because the moral aspirations of white America were too white, too weak, too wedded to the structures of capitalism and worldwide exploitation, partly because no white allies were seeking to create a new counterforce, new pressure points, in their own communities. For all these reasons and many more, the pressure on America was released, and it once again chose not to follow the best and hopeful visions we offered to share.

It is in the light of this very history of hope, of betrayal, of vision and of brokenness that I find my own answer to the essential question. Is America in any sense chosen? So far, in the realm of the nation's most profound contradictions of race and class, America has not chosen to reshape its own origins, its own destiny, to move forward in that humanizing, community-building mission which is the central calling of all children of the earth today. Yet that *no* is not the last word (is it ever?).

Rather, it seems to me that there are at least three more words which must be spoken at this point. The first word is this. In spite of the recent phase of reaction where blacks are concerned, the fact is that after the last two decades in America the black-white relationship can never be the same again. For the power of our own dynamism and the conjoined forces of history have pressed us into new places, new roles, especially in the critical public sector of the society (the sector of the future). Also, the force of our movement has driven us more deeply into the consciousness of the rest of America than ever before. Any struggle to dislodge us entirely from inner or outer positions will open a new stage of America's struggles. We cannot be driven back to where we were.

At the same time, we have seen more of America than ever before. We have recognized with new clarity that more than racial issues are involved in the continued suppression of the masses of our people. We have seen the systemic economic and political levels which must be addressed in the next stages. Some of us have recognized that we must engage in struggle for total change in America if we would rescue the vast majority of our young people from moral destruction and economic obliteration. Thus the single most important bearers of America's inner history are moving to meet the outer history at frightening but necessary borders of encounter, opening new possibilities of vision and choice. Opening as well, of course, new dangers, that we will be sucked into the immoral aspirations of America, crushed by the weight of the very structures we have entered. We live in that perilous dialectic, with hope.

The second of the last words is this: the black movement of our own generation, combined with the war in Vietnam, has produced a new set of black and white forces which are still not clearly enough discerned and still are to be reckoned with. Through our struggle and the related antiwar movement, women and men found training, experience, models and hope. We helped hatch the white radical students who rose out of the 1960's and have flown in many directions. We inspired the latest coming of the women's liberation movement, the gay liberation forces, the welfare rights movement. Our struggle clearly encouraged the native Americans, Chicanos and Asian-Americans to seek out new stages in the struggle against a white-dominated and -defined America. We blacks helped create a new ambience in the prisons, in the armed forces, even in the Communist Party of the United States. All of these are more than groupings, organizations, persons. They represent tendencies, ways of thought, potential for new directions—as well as for tired repetition of old lines.

Still, what I am saying is that our struggle for freedom, for chosenness, for a new America, has actually opened Pandora's box, the pathway to new possibilities. Of course, we do not know what white America will choose, but it clearly cannot effectively choose to follow its nostalgia and fears back into the fifties, back into a dreamland, white-land, free-enterprise, "we're-number-one" land. Never again. Too many persons have begun to raise too many questions. Too many persons have glimpsed a vision of new possibilities.

In a sense, then, many of the component parts of the formerly submerged forces and groups, all those who must eventually participate in any struggle for the creation of a new America, have been aroused by our movement in ways which simply did not exist before now. In a sense, the stage is more ready than ever before for all of us who choose it to begin creating the second coming of America. For the first beginning did not include us, indeed consciously excluded us. In the second coming, we who were the outsiders may choose to become major creators, may studiously avoid the relatively easier path of complaining, protesting victims, may seize the future (against major contending, resisting forces), and shape it. That is the position in which we have placed ourselves through the history we have created in America since World War II. That is the stance made possible by the nonwhite, non-Western revolutions of the last three decades.

This leads us to the third and final word. In spite of the past, because of the past, I think chosenness is still available. As a nation, we are crowded by our past to the edge of history and we cannot turn back. Within this history we have gathered together (through great rivers of blood and tears) an assemblage of nations and peoples unmatched in any single body politic in the world. Indeed, we are, in many ways, a microcosm of the peoples of the world, an earnest of its best and worst possibilities. At terrible human cost we have also gathered the greatest collection of certain kinds of technological expertise, a situation which can provide the setting for attempts at almost anything. Now, with new social forces in array on every hand, all that is lacking is the profoundly human integument to bind these parts together; what is missing is the deeply moral content, the great vision, to build it into a truly new future for the world, whose sign we are.

In the face of this potential, I think that the Hughes-Fuentes-nonwhite challenge and vision still stand. America can be remade by its people, can remold its origins by choosing a new, immensely more human future direction, can redeem its soul by remaking its basic economic, political and spiritual centers.

But at this stage of the nation's history it is very clear that more than poetic rhetoric is required to recreate America, just as more than revolutionary rhetoric was required the first time around. By now, seeing as we have behind the FBI, CIA and massive corporate doors, seeing behind the screens of our own fears and weaknesses, our own cynicism and despair, we know something of what terrible risks, costs and demands are involved, what harrowing journeys into the wilderness of new creation are required.

In a sense, what is needed is a crucial gathering of many kinds of white men and women who are not afraid to take up the historic challenge of the black poets and freedom fighters, to follow the vision of the stones which the builders rejected. In the same way, what is required is the rebuilding and recreation of a critical mass of blacks and other nonwhites who can be called away from America's worst habits to be faithful to their own best creativity and history. What is needed is such men and women who will finally dare to step beyond even the best dreams and visions of others and move to create their own visions of a truly new American society, shaped in the forge of struggle.

All this, of course, must open up slowly, painfully, with individuals who begin to struggle to transform themselves, who consciously search for ways beyond the current cynicism (or the cotton-candy enthusiasms of American presidential elections), who begin to ask what kind of society we need in order to become more human. It begins as such persons reach out to meet others, to study, to encourage, to criticize, to organize, to develop themselves into a new and powerful force. Along the way, they will seek out and discover others who are also choosing to struggle for a new future.

And here is the end of the last word, a caveat. Even if the path of a new America is chosen, a humane America, shaped for human

development in community and not for profits, isolation and lone-
liness, it will surely not make us "the chosen ones" in any of the
older senses of the word. Instead, eventually it will probably break
us out beyond what we have known as "our nation" to join the
advance of humankind's evolution towards the fullest possible development of its own potential.

As long as there are humans in this land, I think America,
Americans, all of us, have the opportunity for chosenness. With
Langston Hughes, I believe America can be. I am committed to
see that America *will* be. In the light of my ancestors, in the face of
my children, I can do no other.

Now, remembering again that we are the celebrants of a special
inner history, here is a final meditation from a black poet, cele-
brating all that dark and dazzling core of men and women and their
thin white line of comrades who chose to be chosen, who died to
make America again.

> Into your palm I place the ashes
> Into your palm are the ashes of your brothers
>   burnt in the Alabama night
> Into your palm that holds your babies
> into your palm that feeds your infants
> into your palm that holds the work tools
> I place the ashes of your father
> here are the ashes of your husbands
> Take the ashes of your nation
> and create the cement to build again
> Create the spirits to move again
> Take this soul dust and begin again.*

---

* Ed Bullins, "Creation Spell," *Journal of Black Poetry* (1969).

American Aspirations and the Grounds of Hope

Theodore M. Hesburgh

American aspiration, like love, is a many-splendored thing. Its roots are deep in the history of this country. In great part, it is the sum of the aspirations of every single American who came to these shores, if they came freely as most did, seeking something splendid, something impossible for them in the land they left. In great part also, the aspirations of Americans are what can be derived from the thoughts, often conflicting, of our Founding Fathers and how these thoughts found expression in our basic documents, the Declaration of Independence and the Constitution. To these two considerations one must add immediately the fact that aspirations, like everything human, tend to evolve, develop and even change over time. History is a safe departure point, but the farther we progress from that primordial starting point, the greater the danger of history being rewritten to fit some modern persuasion or concern or even hope. Revisionism is a favorite indoor sport in these bicentennial days.

I would like to begin on the firmest ground we have available, a shorthand look at the history of those days when America, as we know and love it, really began. In this *tour d'horizon*, I shall merely try to state the facts as they are generally known and accepted. Interpretation comes after the fact.

It is an interesting fact that our Western Hemisphere was one of the last to be known and settled by what was then known as civilized man, which in our prejudiced way comes to read Western man. The fact is that men and women, human beings, had been in our hemisphere somewhere between fifteen and forty millennia before Western man arrived. While we would consider their lifestyle generally primitive, it was, for the longest part of their history, no more primitive than that of most other humans around the world. Somehow they did manage to feed and clothe and organize themselves politically. They also created, in complete isolation, two rather extraordinary civilizations, the Maya in Meso-America and the Inca in the high plateaus of South America.

The Mayas, the oldest and best-civilized people in our hemi-

131

sphere, outlasted the Olmecs, Zapotecas and Teotihuacans. The Mayas were a peaceful people, oligarchically ruled, given to art and architecture, developing a calendar as accurate as ours, but based on Venus which shines most brightly in their southern sky. They had glyphs to record their dates and happenings. The other, more warlike, civilizations, before and after them, came and went more quickly. Maybe there is a lesson in this. When John L. Stevens first reported scientifically on the highly civilized Mayan remains at Chichen-Itza, Uzmal, Palenque, and Tikal in 1841-43, the intellectuals of that time insisted that no native Americans could have created such wonders. There had to be some extraordinary intervention in the dim past from the West or from China. I only mention the Mayas to indicate that the history of this continent did not begin from scratch with the arrival of the Spanish, French, English, or Portuguese. The Mayas were building pyramids and palaces when some of these Europeans were living in caves.

Our story of America, of its aspirations as reflected in the Declaration and the Constitution, really begins with the arrival of two new groups, the English in Virginia and the Pilgrims in New England.* While both settlements were potential disasters, they both became, with all that followed, one of the most significant human and political experiments in the history of mankind.

Before tracing the history of this political development, one should think for a moment about the land that was about to be resettled. Its three million square miles have everything our good planet earth can provide, more useful forest and mineral wealth than any other land, one-half the coal on earth, for example. It is laced with rivers and dotted with lakes, large and small. No country on earth can match its midwestern argicultural lands and climate. Its mountains are both modest and spectacular. It is bounded by the two greatest oceans and felicitously situated between 22′ and 55′ North. Below it are debilitating tropics and above much land that is comparatively bleak and unproductive. Since one cannot reproduce this total magnificent land mass anywhere in the world, perhaps it should not be mentioned in interpreting the meaning of the American experience for the rest of the world. However, it would seem uncritical to recount that experience without at least mentioning the physiognomy of this great

---

* I am indebted to Alistair Cooke's *America* for many of the facts and insights that follow.

land in which it occurred. Land is a given. It may be well or badly used. It is only the spirit and character of a people that eventually shape a land, forge a nation upon it.

Somehow, in our story, the spirit of the people was to match the great goodness and expansiveness of this land. Even so, for our forebears there was, in fact, a great land waiting for nationhood. Once the Virginians and the Pilgrims were in place, granting that they brought with them a great heritage, both positive and negative, events moved quickly as history goes. Remember that the Mayas, our early neighbors, were a thousand years or two developing as a people and their striking civilization flourished from 100 B.C. until a century before the year 1000, when they disintegrated internally and were conquered by the Toltecs. Six hundred years later, when Christopher Columbus and his followers touched these shores, the stage was set for a new experiment. A vast continent was available. Successive waves of people would arrive and a new form of self-government would emerge. It would, like all history, result from what people did and how they were led, how their new aspirations took shape in their new and emerging institutions.

In Virginia, the creative leaders were Thomas Jefferson and Patrick Henry and the institutions, formal and informal, were the House of Burgesses and the Raleigh Tavern. In Massachusetts, John Winthrop was the man and the Mayflower Compact gave rise to a basic form of self-government that grew quickly under Governor Winthrop's leadership. One might note for future reference that Winthrop wanted to create a city of God, originally in Ireland, then in Virginia which he fortuitously missed by bad navigation, giving him the chance to form independently the Massachusetts Bay Colony. It should also be noted that before they had a say in government through election, these people had to be certified as God's elect. Also, the new liberties were only for Puritans at first, not others.

Within a year of his arrival, Winthrop's government had guaranteed trial by jury, protection of life and property by due process, freedom from self-incrimination, and no taxes for nonvoters. Fortunately, the lowly cod made the colony economically viable, as tobacco did in Virginia.

As we begin to speak of the American experience, it should be remembered that we are referring to thirteen different colonies spread thinly along 1,400 miles of Atlantic coastline. These thirteen colonies were like thirteen nations, each with its own government, currency, trade laws, and special religious customs. What was special about them, even as colonies, were their town meetings, their having elected rather than appointed state militias, their abolition of primogeniture, and, in general, their freedom. Curiously, for those early years, what really bound the thirteen together was their allegiance to the King of England until George III upset the applecart.

When George III tried to make the colonists pay for the expenses of the Franco-British war in America, by the Stamp Act, the reaction on this side of the Atlantic was violent. When, through unusual political stupidity, all the taxes were revoked except that on tea, which almost everybody drank, there was a series of events that all remember: the Boston Massacre, the Tea Party, the meeting in Old South Church. This revolution was conceived in the name of freedom and liberty—heady notions for colonists.

The colonial underground with its Committees of Correspondence was formed and Sam Adams, the leader of the Boston Tea Party, called for a Continental Congress with Thomas Jefferson and Patrick Henry aiding and abetting from Raleigh Tavern in Virginia.

Again, the distant British government overreacted. The Port of Boston—a vital colonial economic lifeline—was closed and General Thomas Gage dispatched there with four regiments of troops. In Williamsburg, Virginia, the House of Burgesses was closed. They would have done better to close Raleigh Tavern and South Church.

The denouement came quickly with the Philadelphia meeting of the rebels and the choosing of 43-year-old George Washington as Continental Commander, following Lexington, Concord, and the "shot heard around the world" in April of 1775.

It is amazing how great documents are sometimes composed in humble circumstances. At the beginning of the hot summer of 1776, five remarkable early Americans gathered in a room over a horse stable in Philadelphia. One thinks of the smell and the horseflies. These five men represented in microcosm the three cultures of the thirteen colonies: John Adams of the Puritan oligarchy of New England, with Roger Sherman of Connecticut, Benjamin Franklin of Pennsylvania, and Robert Livingston of New York representing the mercantile middle colonies, and Thomas Jefferson, the great Southern aristocrat, who at the age of thirty-three wrote the stirring final draft.

I suppose it can be fairly said that more than anything else the Declaration of Independence continues to state the deepest aspirations of the American people. The Declaration was dated on the fourth of July, but published a day earlier. Later, fifty-six greats would sign and endorse it, thus pledging their lives, fortunes, and sacred honor for the revolutionary ideas the Declaration now proclaimed to all the world. The signers were not really revolutionary types, although they had the spirit of a new creation, as Crevecoeur put it, "this new man." John Hancock signed at the top with a bold flourish so that, as he said, "The King of England could read it without his glasses."

If the world was to be shaken, then and in the years to come, it would be because of two basic revolutionary statements:

That all men are created equal, that they are endowed by their Creator with certain unalienable rights, that among these are life, liberty, and the pursuit of happiness.

That to secure these rights, governments are instituted among men, deriving their just powers from the consent of the governed.

Nothing could be more alien political doctrine in the lands and traditions of monarchy from which the ancestors of these men came a short century and a half before. In the years ahead, and in the centuries that followed, these same revolutionary ideas would help to end monarchical France, the German Empire, Imperial Russia, and, in our lifetime, colonies all around the world.

Five years later, on October 19, 1781, Lord Cornwallis surrendered to the rabble army, so-called, at Yorktown. In 1783, the peace treaty was signed in Paris.

But the country was far from being really born. The committee to draft the Articles of Confederation had begun work nine days after the Declaration of Independence. By 1781, these Articles were the Law of Congress, but they simply produced what was called the "Disunited States of America," all the states going their own merry way, the Congress being the only national institution.

The fatal flaw was to attempt to establish a national government while leaving to the states ultimate sovereignty. This reminds us somewhat of the plight of the United Nations today.

The Declaration had declared rights and liberty, but it did not specify the form of government under which these were to be secured. There was an exalted end, a high purpose, in clear view, but no effective instrument of government to achieve the dream of the Declaration.

Happily, fifty-five of the Founding Fathers were again called together in 1787 in Philadelphia, at the State House now called Independence Hall. The Fathers were the most civilized of the revolutionaries, the elite of government, business, and the professions in the various states. Half of them were lawyers; more than half college graduates. Their average age was forty-two. Again, unlikely revolutionaries.

The task before them was stark and simple: how to establish a government that, unlike the Articles of Confederation, would effectively balance the power between the central government and the states. How to do it was not so simple, although they completed their work in seventeen weeks.

In general, they knew what they were against: monarchy and standing armies which were almost always used to suppress freedom. They wanted a republic, but what kind? George Washington, as chairman, used his considerable prestige to hold the convention together—in secrecy no less—and focused on the central issue which was argued from two extremes. Alexander Hamilton, the protagonist of the aristocratic principle, wanted a very strong central government that could veto the states which he would have preferred to eliminate altogether. Hamilton also wanted a president and Senate elected for life. George Mason of Virginia, twice Hamilton's age, argued the other extreme. Mason wanted the weakest central government possible, consonant with confederacy. Having previously drawn up the Virginia Bill of Rights, he wanted a similar bill for America, with his favorite rights of freedom from search without a warrant, freedom of assembly, and no double jeopardy under the law included. Neither Hamilton nor Mason won the day, Mason even losing his Bill of Rights, though this was to come later.

The mediator who saved the day and made the Constitution possible was James Madison, thirty-six, also of Virginia. For

Madison, true to the Declaration, the main purpose of government was "to act upon and for the individual citizen," protecting minorities from the majority, granting no states' rights above the central government. Madison's key dictum was that if men were virtuous, there would be no need for governments at all. Taking a dimmer view than Jefferson's about human virtue, he suggested a government of checks and balances, with separate branches of government responsible to different constituencies. In this, he was faithfully following Montesquieu. He was willing to let these separate powers collide for their own good political health, with a president to keep an eye on Congress, a Congress to keep an eye on the president, and a Supreme Court to keep an eye on both of them. The Supreme Court is the key here since its concern is not for precedents of common law, but, purely and simply, for the Constitution which controls the legitimacy of both presidential and congressional action. He would have the national government represent all variety of men, interests, and factions.

The Convention decided that to achieve balance, all states would have two senators and a proportionate number of representatives in the House for lesser terms to represent the grass roots, as it were. The national government, the source of national unity, would neither coerce nor rival the states. All powers not stipulated for the purposes of national government would devolve on the states which would control such matters as education, highways, taxation, banking, liquor laws, criminal and civil codes. Without this last concession, the states would have left the Convention.

So the Constitution evolved in the weeks that followed and was ultimately adopted by the states, though not without difficulty. The vote in Virginia, for example, was eighty-nine for and seventy-nine against, Patrick Henry and George Mason voting against.

The historic drama was not quite finished. Thomas Jefferson, who as minister to France was not in the Convention, heard of Mason's failure to get the Bill of Rights. Jefferson felt that the Constitution, as written, was a good political document, but imperfect without a specific guarantee of the rights for which all of them had fought and separated themselves from the crown. He urged twenty such basic rights—the true specific aspirations of all Americans—and within four years, ten amendments were passed comprising most of his twenty and allowing for others to come. In fact, sixteen more have been added to the original ten, and we are presently considering others. It may well be that Jefferson, too, saved the day because the Constitution, without the Bill of Rights, may just not have been workable, especially as the Constitution became more detached in men's minds from the Declaration, the clarion call for liberty. The Constitution along with the Bill of Rights was the engine created to make the aspirations and promise of the Declaration of Independence come true. That promise has been 200 years in the making.

I suppose it is quite natural as America grew and prospered, and entered quite lately the wider world of all mankind and all human striving, that increasingly it is asked what the Founding Fathers really meant and how well they spoke for the aspirations of Americans, not only then, but yet today. It is also being questioned that they really spoke to the world at all. These are perhaps unfair questions, but they are being asked and should be answered.

One of the best responses to these questions comes from a recent issue of *Public Interest* (Fall, 1975) especially prepared for the bicentennial. The focus of these articles written by scholars of congenial concern is to react to modern America in the light of Lord Bryce's classic, *The American Commonwealth,* published in 1888, shortly after the first centennial celebration. All was not well in 1876, but considerably improved a dozen years later when Lord Bryce wrote in his work:

> The institutions of the United States are deemed by inhabitants and admitted by strangers to be a matter of more general interest than those of not less famous nations of the Old World. They are, or are supposed to be, institutions of a new type. They form, or are supposed to form, a symmetrical whole, capable of being studied and judged together more profitably than the less perfectly harmonized institutions of older countries. They represent an experiment in the rule of the multitude, tried on a scale unprecedentedly vast, and the results of which everyone is concerned to watch. And yet they are something more than an experiment, for they are believed to disclose and display the type of institutions towards which, as by a law of fate, the rest of civilized mankind are forced to move, some with swifter, others with slower, but all with unresting feet.

In the vernacular of today's youth, the response of these scholars writing in *Public Interest* is "no way." Daniel Patrick Moynihan leads the procession in his introduction when he says of the world today that the American experiment in democracy is not going very well. "Neither liberty nor democracy would seem to be prospering —or in any event neither would seem to have a future—nearly as auspicious as their past." As to others following our lead, he adds: "To the contrary, liberal democracy on the American model increasingly tends to the condition of monarchy in the nineteenth century; a hold-over form of government which persists in isolated or particular places here and there, and which may even serve well enough for special circumstances, but which has no relevance for the future. It is where the world was, not where it is going."

It is true, as Moynihan observes, that we held the field during much of the nineteenth century and reached a kind of apogee with Woodrow Wilson in 1919, then to be challenged by all forms of socialist regimes, some or even most now masquerading under the name of democratic republics. Of our own patriotic stance, Moynihan says: "The flag remains, but little else that is not battered or banal or both." He has for us only one last word of hope, more reminiscent of Greek political philosophy than of Locke or Montesquieu: "For when all else is gone, virtue remains. If it has ever existed, it is present still."

On this slim reed of hope, I would base my disagreement with him and most of the authors of this volume, insofar as they too often exude an all-permeating pessimism on the future of America or of America's aspirations. Most of what they say is true, but there are various ways of interpreting the truth, especially as one looks to the future in a bicentennial year. Lord Bryce could not have been quite so expansive had he written a dozen years earlier, at the time of the first centennial. History brings problems, but also new hope and new perspectives. All is not lost, despite the current pessimism of many intellectuals.

As a sagacious Frenchman once wrote: "At each epoch of history the world was in a hopeless state, and at each epoch of history, the world muddled through; at each epoch, the world was lost, and at each epoch, it was saved" (Jacques Maritain, *Reflections on America*). One hopes that this is still true today.

However, before hoping for the best, one should look to the worst. This is very briefly what the authors in the special issue of *Public Interest* reflect.

The opening essay by Samuel Huntington says that the democratic circuits are presently overcharged by the demands of minority and other special interest groups. He believes, if I read him correctly, that they demand more than democracy can deliver and they demand it here and now and all at once. Unless they learn to moderate their demands, democracy overindulged will become a threat to America. He quotes John Adams to say that "Democracy never lasts long. It soon wastes, exhausts, and murders itself. There never was a democracy that did not commit suicide." Huntington adds: "A value which is good in itself is not necessarily optimized when it is maximized . . . there are potentially desirable limits to the extension of political democracy. Democracy could have a longer life if it has a more balanced existence."

Another author, Martin Diamond, is seized by the idea that modern academics have reversed the Founding Fathers' idea of liberty as the goal and democracy as the means to attain it. Democracy has been transformed into the uniform litmus paper of our worldwide approval or disapproval of governments, an ideology "of equality in every respect." As he says it, "The underlying complaint against the American political order is no longer a matter of mere reforms, or even of wholesale constitutional revision, although there is always a kind of itch in that direction, but rather a critique of the entire regime in the name of a demand for equality in every aspect of human life. It is a demand which consists in a kind of absolutization of a single principle, the principle of equality, and at the same time of an absolutization of the democratic form of government understood as the vehicle for that complete equality. This is a different posture towards democracy indeed than that embodied in the American founding." Diamond is raising the question whether liberty or egalitarianism is the prime goal of America, and whether democracy, which is not even mentioned in the Constitution, is to be taken as a means or an end.

A whole spate of authors who follow say that America is ready for a decentralization of political power, and a lowering of utopian morality, especially worldwide, a realization that the American government cannot do everything.

The final essay of the series by Daniel Bell reiterates a common theme, that America has had a loss of innocence and is now coming of age with a sense of its mortality and fallibility. Bell concludes:

> The recent political history of the successive administrations has left the nation with much moral disrepute. All of this places a great

responsibility on the leadership of the society. This necessitates the recreation of a moral credibility whose essential condition is simple honesty and openness. It means the conscious commitment in foreign policy to limit the national power to purposes proportionate with national interest, and to forego any hegemonic dream, even of being the moral policeman of the world. Domestically it means the renewed commitment to the policy of inclusion whereby disadvantaged groups have priority in social policy, both as an act of justice, and to diffuse social tensions that could explode. The act of "conscious will" has to replace the wavering supports of American exceptionalism as the means of holding the society together.

Of all the gifts bestowed on this country at its founding, the one that alone remains as the element of American exceptionalism is the constitutional system, with a comity that has been undergirded by history. And it is the recognition of history, now that the future has receded, which provides the meaning of becoming twice-born. America was the exemplary once-born nation, the land of sky-blue optimism in which the traditional ills of civilization were, as Emerson once said, merely the measles and whooping cough of growing up. The act of becoming twice-born, the entrance into maturity, is the recognition of mortality of countries within the time scales of history.

I should apologize for interpreting so much from so little, but I did read the articles in question carefully, and do conclude that the last thing the American people, and indeed the world, need in this bicentennial year is more pessimism. Granted we are at a difficult juncture in the history of mankind, and are at times reminded of Ronald Knox's jingle:

God's world had a hopeful beginning
But man marred his chances by sinning
We hope that the story
Will end in God's glory
But at present the other side's winning.

If man needs one commodity today more than anything else it is hope. Despite all America's flaws, and today we are in a paroxysm to exhibit all in detail, the simple fact is that America and her aspirations are still today the best expression of what I would call mankind's universal hope.

John Nef terminated his book, *The United States and Civilization,* with a similar thought, paraphrasing together both Rousseau and Marx. "Goodness and wisdom were born free, but everywhere they are in chains. Good people, honorable people, intelligent people, truth-loving people of the world, unite. You have nothing material to gain for yourselves; but you have the opportunity to serve humanity. You have the opportunity to bring about a rebirth of the human mind and spirit."

Such a rebirth will not occur, even in our times, if the American experience fails, which is to say, if we lose heart. We, as a people, said Lincoln, were conceived in liberty and dedicated to the proposition that all men are created equal. Few, if any, bodies politic began quite this way or lasted quite this long under an inspired Constitution. Few, if any, countries have received so many miserable people, over so brief a span of time, and inspired them so quickly with a common ideal and a common task of achieving liberty and justice for all. No country has such a variegated population representing every nationality, color, culture and religion on earth.

America has more blacks than there are Canadians in Canada, more Spanish-speaking than Australians in Australia, more American Indians than when Columbus arrived, two or three times more Jews than Israel.

During the 1840's and 1850's more than a fourth of the population of Ireland came to America when a million died in Ireland during the Potato Famine. Before 1890, the largest influx of immigrants was from Germany, Scandinavia, England and Ireland, afterwards from Italy, Austria, Hungary, Russia, Poland and just about everywhere else. In the first two decades of this century, over fourteen and a half million persons passed through Ellis Island, at times 8000 a day, with 15,000 waiting in New York Harbor, mostly illiterate, most possessing only the required $25, but all filled with limitless new hope.

Somehow they all learned to live together, with increasing comity and tolerance and, one should add, the kind of virtue that only such an unusual situation could elicit. In a sense, our American population, like no other on earth, represents the spread, the variety, as well as the yearnings of universal humanity. If we cannot press forward to achieve these basic aspirations of liberty, equality and fraternity—to borrow from the French—in a government that Lincoln best described as "of the people, by the people, for the people," I do not know what other nation is likely to do so on such a scale and with such a *dramatis personae* as America possesses.

Again, Lincoln put it best in his First Inaugural message, speaking of the basic American aspiration: "The struggle for maintaining in the world that form and substance of government whose leading object is to elevate the condition of men; to lift artificial weights from all shoulders; to clear the paths of laudable pursuit for all; to afford all an unfettered start and a fair chance in the race of life."

Lincoln was under no illusion that America's experiment was complete, a closed book. In fact, he was facing the greatest contradiction and flaw in our history, slavery. It is a curious fact that even the Founding Fathers could not honestly solve this dilemma. There was to have been a brave denunciation of slavery in the Declaration of Independence, but it was deleted at the insistence of Southern slave owners and Northern shippers. In the Articles of Confederation, the quota of troops was specified in proportion to the *white* population at the insistence of the South. During the discussion on the Constitution, a Southerner, George Mason, proposed to abolish slavery, but was defeated. Almost a century passed before the nation went to war on the issue.

When Lincoln proposed the Emancipation Proclamation, his whole cabinet voted nay. Lincoln voted aye and remarked, "The ayes have it." The Proclamation emerged during the Civil War in 1863. But even then, even after the end of the war and the passage of the Thirteenth, Fourteenth, and Fifteenth Amendments, the matter was not settled. President Hayes sold out the blacks to gain the South and the presidency. The nation took a monumental step backwards as the Reconstruction ingloriously ended. Even the Supreme Court capped it with *Plessy-Fergusson*.

Over a half century passed until the Supreme Court began to undo the damage with the *Brown* decision in 1954. President Eisenhower then remarked that his appointment of Earl Warren as chief justice was one of his great mistakes. In fact, little happened. In the next decade, less than 3 percent of the *de jure* dual school systems of the South were integrated. It took another Southerner, Lyndon Johnson, to complete what Missourian Harry Truman had begun by integrating the armed forces after World War II. Johnson really pushed the Congress after Kennedy's assassination to pass the landmark Civil Rights Acts of 1964, 1965 and 1968.

In the one short decade of the sixties this nation, at long last, corrected the injustices and indignities of more than three centuries, granting American blacks equality of opportunity in voting, education, employment, housing, administration of justice, political participation and public accommodations. The latter, following the passage of the 1964 omnibus Civil Rights Act, overturned in one day vicious laws and customs dating back to the arrival of the first black slave in then white America.

I submit that no nation, ever, has accomplished more in a decade for human rights and the ultimate vindication of justice than America did in the decade of the sixties. This action was more important by far as a positive step forward than the negative actions of Vietnam and Watergate. It is also a reason for hope of what might yet be accomplished.

I believe that at least this illustrates in the modern context the truism that the battle for freedom and equality, for life, liberty and the pursuit of happiness is never truly won. Each generation of Americans, indeed of all humanity, must strive to achieve these aspirations anew. Liberty is a living flame to be fed, not dead ashes to be revered, even in a bicentennial year. The world at large is ever conscious of what is happening in America, good and evil. They are even more conscious of what we are doing to make our aspirations work, here or wherever in the world we do business or diplomacy.

It was no mistake or accident of history that after World War II, an American and a Frenchman, a woman and a man, a Christian and a Jew, Eleanor Roosevelt and René Cassin, authored the Universal Declaration of Human Rights. It is a shame that so few important nations, ourselves included, have ever officially approved the two great United Nations Protocols that flowed from this Declaration—that of political and civil rights, and that of economic, social and cultural rights. It would be a great and symbolic act to do so in our bicentennial year. I believe deeply that these statements of human rights represent the truest aspirations of Americans and of humankind generally. We must lead the way today, as we did at the time of our nation's birth. We might also push, at this time, for the appointment of a United Nations High Commissioner of Human Rights, to be the conscience of the world in this most important and, today, highly violated area.

As Madame de Stael told a Boston scholar in 1817, "You are the advance guard of the human race." Ten years later, Goethe remarked, "Amerika, du hast es besser als unser Kontinent." A century later, in the early hours of the morning of November 11, 1918, the day of the Armistice, Woodrow Wilson wrote: "Everything for which America has fought has been accomplished. It will now be our fortunate duty to assist by example, by sober friendly counsel and by material aid in the establishment of just democracy throughout the world." Sailing for France and the Peace Conference, he said: "We are to be an instrument in the hands of God to see that liberty is made secure for mankind." An impossible dream for those days perhaps, when America turned inward and rejected the League of Nations, but again we did better in avoiding isolationism and creating new international organizations after the next world war. Anyway, the aspirations for liberty, justice and peace lived on, despite the dismal decade of the twenties.

In a turnabout of history, Franklin Roosevelt said that he was sending arms to a beleaguered Britain "to enable them to fight for their liberty and our security. We have the men, the skill, the wealth, and, above all, the will. We must be the great arsenal of democracy."

Finally, two decades and a half after World War II, John Kennedy continued the presidential expression of our national aspirations, during a cold war, for all the world to hear in his inaugural: "Let every nation know, whether it wishes us well or ill, that we shall pay any price, bear any burden, meet any hardship, support any friend, oppose any foe, to assure the survival and the success of liberty."

Is all of this empty rhetoric, or is it a constant tradition, from the Declaration of 200 years ago, that still speaks of liberty to the heart of our people and to the world? I, for one, do not believe that America is a thwarted experiment, a burned-out case, a fading hope. Despite the negativism of the day, we are becoming "twice-born," coming of age, and it is not the decrepitude of old age. A wise man once said that liberty is the luxury of self-discipline. We do indeed need much more self-discipline in America today. The world may or may not follow, but we must lead because our tradition says we must; liberty is worth the effort, and the creation of justice and peace abroad will in large measure depend on the measure of justice and peace that we create here at home. Whatever its faults, America is still the most exciting human experiment in all the world.

Sometimes, in the heat and even despair of the constant struggle to live up to our aspirations, in an increasingly complex and mud-

dled world, it might raise our spirits and deepen our faith and hope
to see ourselves as others see us. My concluding lines were written
by a French philosopher, Jacques Maritain, in America, in 1943,
when his home country, under the Nazi heel, was anything but
free:

> There is indeed one thing that Europe knows and knows only
> too well; that is the tragic significance of life. . . . There is one
> thing that America knows well and that she teaches as a great and
> precious lesson to those who come in contact with her astounding
> adventure: it is the value and dignity of the common man, the
> value and dignity of the people. . . . America knows that the
> common man has a right to the "pursuit of happiness"; the pursuit
> of the elementary conditions and possessions which are the pre-
> requisites of a free life, and the denial of which, suffered by such
> multitudes, is a horrible wound in the flesh of humanity; the
> pursuit of the higher possessions of culture and the spirit. . . . Here
> heroism is required, not to overcome tragedy, but to bring to a
> successful conclusion the formidable adventure begun in this
> country with the Pilgrim Fathers and the pioneers, and continued
> in the great days of the Declaration of Independence and the
> Revolutionary War (*Reflections on America*).

Afterword

I

There are many common strains and some interesting differences that stand out in the preceding essays. It seems most appropriate to focus attention on those points that touch the theme of the conference which brought together the contributors to this volume. If there are any national moral aspirations that are yet alive and command wide support in America, they are found in what are set down as the self-evident truths of the Declaration of Independence. Although denying that the Declaration functioned that way at the time of the Revolution, Marshall Smelser writes approvingly of Lincoln's making it "the moral basis of the republic" and concludes by describing it as "the testament of American ideals" honored by later generations. Alfred Kazin refers to the Declaration as the statement of America's "positive ideals," and Sydney Ahlstrom, following Chesterton, finds the "soul" of America in the Declaration's creed.

Like Lincoln himself, Theodore Hesburgh and Martin Diamond look to both the Declaration and the Constitution as America's testament, the locus of American aspirations. Yet, as in the case of Lincoln, the Declaration's more profound and hence more fundamental role is acknowledged. Father Hesburgh writes that the Declaration "continues to state the deepest aspirations of the American people." Martin Diamond notes that the Declaration tells of "the deepest stratum of American political life" and that the Declaration settles much, for "in a crucial way" it " 'popularizes' the whole of political life."

Recognition of the Declaration's creed as the continuing source of America's most important aspirations is more evident in these essays than explicit acceptance of the universal implications of that creed and a unique American role in the realization of those aspirations worldwide. Such acceptance is clearest in Father Hesburgh's insistence "that America and her aspirations are still today the best expression of . . . mankind's universal hope" and in his call for American leadership in seeking worldwide recognition and protection of human rights. I. Bernard Cohen sees the need for more rather than less science in order to cope with the world's major

147

problems, especially that of "the normal support of life"; he calls
on America to continue the leadership of the world scientific effort
that marked the 1960's. Vincent Harding, pleading against the
slipping back from the achievement in law and awareness that came
in the same 1960's with the successes of the civil rights movement,
calls on Americans to be faithful to the best of their history. This
nation, reborn to be its very best, would be but joining others in the
making of a "new future for the world." However, he argues, this
nation is in a position to "make a signal contribution to the central
human concerns for community and integrity, for justice and
equality, especially where the complex and harrowing issue of race
is concerned."

Most of the essays here do, in fact, resonate with the suggestion
that the American experience and the American responsibility are
more than ordinarily significant for all mankind. This sense of
American specialness seems far indeed from any literal biblical
notion of being "chosen," as that invoked by the Puritans. In fact
this volume at some points suggests the view that American specialness is simply tied to the abundance and power that America enjoys.
However, most contributors to this volume, reflecting a dominant
view among Americans and many observers of America, are quite
close to Lincoln's sense of the term "chosen" when he invoked the
phrase "his almost chosen people."

Lincoln used that phrase on his journey to inauguration in
February of 1861. The Union that Lincoln sought so much to save
was already well into the process of deep division. Jefferson Davis
would be inaugurated as President of the Confederacy while
Lincoln journeyed by rail toward Washington, a city that many feared
was not safe for his own inauguration. Lincoln's relative silence
during the presidential campaign and the period following election
was broken as he faced audiences numerous times a day, first in
leaving Springfield, then crossing Indiana, Ohio, dipping into
western Pennsylvania, returning to Ohio to follow the route through
Cleveland, Erie and into the northwestern corner of New York and
then finally in making his way to the great "commercial city" of
that state. Despite the crumbling of the Union around him, Lincoln
spoke nondivisively and tolerantly. He clearly was interested in
building personal support in the North for whatever decisions he
might have to make, but he seemed to be addressing his remarks to
those who felt threatened by him as well as those generally sup-

portive audiences before him. He spoke many pleasantries, but he also spoke about the Constitution, its processes that had resulted in his recent election and the Union which it secured.

He did not mention the Declaration of Independence in these nine days of speechmaking, even though the Declaration had been the foundation of his position in the Lincoln-Douglas debates and in much of the early speechmaking that brought him to national attention and cast him up as a threat in some areas of the country. In fact, scarcely an indirect reference to the Declaration can be found until in New York City he said that "there is nothing that can ever bring me willingly to consent to the destruction of this Union, . . . unless it were to be that thing for which the Union itself was made." A day later in an address to the New Jersey Senate at Trenton, Lincoln sorted out even more clearly the relationships among the polestars of his political viewpoint. Having reflected on the hardships of the Revolutionary War, he added:

> I am exceedingly anxious that that thing which they struggled for; that something *even more* than National Independence; that something *that held out promise to all people of the world to all time to come;* I am exceedingly anxious that this Union, the Constitution, and the liberties of the people shall be perpetuated in accordance *with the original idea* for which that struggle was made, and I shall be most happy indeed if I shall be an humble instrument in the hands of the Almighty, and of this, *his almost chosen people,* for perpetuating the object of that great struggle. [Emphases are mine.]

On the next day, Washington's birthday, and in Independence Hall at Philadelphia, Lincoln would return to these themes and would unequivocally and explicitly invoke the Declaration of Independence, calling it the source of all his political feelings. If Americans were "chosen," they were, in Lincoln's view, chosen to struggle to make the truths of "the original idea," of the Declaration of Independence, live in their own land and in doing so to hold out "promise to all people of the world."

Lincoln's sense of America's specialness was not at all novel. Although the notion of Americans as "a chosen people" has been and continues to be used in a number of ways—from the original Puritan sense that their American settlement was the beginning of the spiritual regeneration of mankind, to emphases on the blessings

of the American land and location, and even to the more recent
focus on American pluralism and the "melting pot" as microcosm of
the community of man—ways that often overlap and merge
together, Lincoln drew upon the clearly dominant sense among
America's founding statesmen of what it meant for this nation to be
"chosen." And the preceding essays give witness that it remains
the dominant sense yet today.

Leading Americans as well as leading Europeans of the late
eighteenth century looked to the New World, especially with respect
to political and social forms, to realize the Enlightenment that, as
Henry Steele Commager has said, "the Old World imagined." Both
Ahlstrom's and Kazin's essays point out how America in 1776 was
seen as the peak of and the first complete opportunity for the
progressive and revolutionary movements springing from two
hundred years of struggle in Europe. Both essays, but especially
Ahlstrom's, show the easy confluence of Enlightenment aspirations
with those of the Puritans and the other religious separatists who
gave early America so much vigor. "America as Nature, Nature
as Beneficence, Man as the crown of Nature." Thus, writes Alfred
Kazin, America was "man's second chance" and, in Jefferson's
words, "the world's best hope."

That sense of America as "the lead society" pervaded the founding era. In words Benjamin Franklin used during the Revolution,
the American cause is the "Cause of Liberty" and that is the
"Cause of all Mankind." In 1776, Franklin had proposed for the
seal of the United States the depiction of Moses lifting his wand and
dividing the Red Sea while the Pharaoh was swamped by its waters.
Jefferson suggested the portrayal of the children of Israel being led
through the wilderness by a cloud during the day and a pillar of
fire at night. Years later, upon the deaths of Adams and Jefferson,
Daniel Webster would echo Thomas Paine's view of the Revolution
in saying that "it cannot be denied, but by those who would dispute
against the sun, that with America, and in America, a new era
commences in human affairs." At the Constitutional Convention in
1787, the learned James Wilson looked upon the American system
of government as laying "a foundation for erecting temples of
liberty in every part of the earth."

George Washington turned to this theme in his First Inaugural
address, saying that "the preservation of the sacred fire of liberty
and the destiny of the republican model of government are justly

considered, perhaps, as *deeply*, as *finally*, staked on the experiment intrusted to the hands of the American people." Earlier, in 1783, Washington had written about the auspicious time in which America was striving to lay new political foundations. This was not a time, wrote Washington, "of ignorance and superstition"; rather it was "an epoch when the rights of mankind were better understood and more clearly defined, than at any other period. The researches of the human mind after social happiness have been carried to a great extent. . . ." The more spirited Jefferson, in his final assessment of the significance of the Revolution, described it as "the signal of arousing men to burst the chains under which monkish ignorance and superstition had persuaded them to bind themselves, and to assume the blessings and security of self-government." A few years earlier, he had commented to John Adams that if "the cloud of barbarism and despotism again obscure the science and liberties of Europe, this country remains to preserve and restore light and liberty to them."

Lincoln clearly stood in this dominant tradition of Jefferson and other leading founders when he made, again and again in a variety of ways, the claim that this nation was "chosen" to carry out a political experiment for the benefit of all mankind. That experiment was based on the truths of the Declaration of Independence, on a commitment to a common life "conceived in liberty and dedicated to the proposition that all men are created equal." Much, one is tempted to say nearly all, of modern America's self-criticism and hence of American moral aspirations takes a form true to the Declaration and to these words of Lincoln in setting down at Gettysburg the nature of the American commitment. Americans often, at their moral best, worry about faithfulness to that commitment; they measure themselves and others on a scale of achievement in liberty and equality. Such American characteristics are most in evidence in the preceding essays of Vincent Harding and Father Hesburgh.

A more remarkable feature of all these essays and the more necessary stimulus to the political thinking of Americans are found in some of the questions directly and indirectly raised about the possible limitations of the creed of the Declaration or of the prevailing way of understanding and implementing that special yet universal American commitment. Put simply, the essays contain protests against the extremes of an asocial libertarianism and an enthusiastic egalitarianism. As a whole, they raise the question, posed in a way by Sydney Ahlstrom's closing sentence, as to what shall be the terms on which the dialectic of liberty and equality can find a satisfactory synthesis.

Ahlstrom himself is the one who most emphatically points the finger at libertarianism, finding the American Revolution and the earlier Puritan revolution as libertarian revolutions giving rise to and spurring a tradition of excessive individualism in America. The outcome, in his words, is a languishing sense of "distributive justice" and "the general welfare." Alfred Kazin's target seems much the same, for he traces America's earliest and mainstream moral aspirations to the "ego system" against which so many twentieth-century American writers have revolted.

Martin Diamond's striking concern here is with checking the use of the Declaration to support efforts at establishing equality in all realms and at making "democracy and equality the end of human existence itself." The true American tradition, informed by both the Declaration (properly read) and "the new political science" in the Constitution, is one of a "sober and cautious posture" toward equality. This tradition, argues Diamond, insists only on *equal* political liberty; inequalities of other sorts are to be allowed. In fact, some inequalities are necessitated by the commitment to equal political liberty; in Diamond's words, "whoever says equality of liberty thereby says inequality of outcomes." A problem not directly addressed by Diamond is that unequal outcomes (the effects of libertarianism) encroach in various ways on equality of liberty and so arises an egalitarian dynamism, all in the name of equal liberty, not necessarily in the name of equality across-the-board. Diamond, however, takes his stand with equal political *liberty* as a workable and respectable end for government in modern society.

Peter Berger's and I. Bernard Cohen's essays contain more specific indictments of egalitarianism in America. The latter calls for a maturity of judgment on the part of Americans with respect to the funding of scientific research. What Cohen finds in the present scene is "a confusion of values and judgments" with respect to science's role in the American republic. More significant is that this is the general historical picture he gives of the republic's treatment of science; that general picture stands in contrast to the vigorous interest in and support for science in the Revolutionary period and among the republic's founders. That overall picture is also the backdrop for the major role in world scientific leadership that America came to play in the 1960's; it turns out that Cold War competition and sheer abundance, not a maturing democratic judgment, thrust America into that now-fading leadership position. Citing the analysis of Simon Newscomb, a noted astronomer of the nineteenth century, Cohen seems to fix the cause for the republic's poor appreciation of science in the American public's view that cultivation of intellectual excellence is not within the field of this nation's mission. That analysis has, of course, bearing on other forms of higher learning in America.

Peter Berger's quarrels with egalitarianism involve issues even more at the surface of contemporary American society. He questions the wisdom of "court-enforced busing programs" aimed at realizing racial integration in the schools, and he raises serious questions about the tendency of public policy to encroach on the liberty of private associations and, in general, to favor public agencies over private ones in the spheres of welfare, health, and education. Here he stands in contrast to Vincent Harding's approving insistence that the public sector of society is the sector of the future.

Berger's concrete instances of what he regards as misdirected policies are only meant to exemplify the larger case he stakes out. That case is directed, above all, at the dominant way modern America has attempted to achieve liberty and equality and somewhat at a related, if often implicit, tendency to suppose that human happiness is found in the achievement of liberty and equality. This way is the "universalistic" approach characteristic of the Enlightenment. Recognizing much good in this approach, Berger nonetheless feels that the present danger is that it will be carried to a destructive extreme. In political terms, the universalistic approach translates into an overall view that looks only to the state and a mass of individuals, free and equal individuals when things are at their best. In the name of rational procedures, this approach favors centralization and increasingly it favors centralization in the public sector; this occurs at the expense of what Berger calls "mediating structures"; such mediating "communities and communal institutions" are squeezed out in the name of the efficient pursuit of liberty and equality. This threatens, argues Berger, the social and political health of a free society, for it is the mediating institutions—namely, family, church, voluntary association, neighborhood and subculture

—that are necessary if the individual is to avoid a personally destructive sense of *anomie* and if the society is to have effective means of generating and maintaining a common moral conscience.

So Berger joins others here in questioning the adequacy of the Declaration's creed as well as the way America understands her commitment to liberty and equality and the means she uses to pursue those goals. Nor are the essays of Father Hesburgh and Vincent Harding free from the suggestion that the simple commitment to liberty and equality is not a wholly adequate statement of what American moral aspirations must be. "Justice" keeps breaking into the language of Father Hesburgh as a measure of future aspirations, and Harding's call for justice and "new levels" of community and human life evokes a notion of a much more profound regeneration than would be entailed in a recommitment to the Declaration's truths. At another point Father Hesburgh reminds his readers that "liberty is the luxury of self-discipline" and that "much more self-discipline" is needed in today's America.

Alexis de Tocqueville, recalls Martin Diamond in his essay, once looked to America as the "paradigmatic experiment in democratic liberty." Father Hesburgh recalls Lincoln's view that the American experiment was not complete; later Father Hesburgh looks upon it as "still the most exciting human experiment in all the world." The posture of these essays does point out how open and continuing the American experiment is. It is clear that the experiment, especially in the context of a modernized urban society existing in an increasingly interdependent world, cannot be conceived simply in terms of how faithful the nation can be to liberty and equality. The experiment does, now more than ever, involve the necessity of intelligently confronting the question of the meaning, and thus the limits, of liberty and equality as the common goals of this "almost chosen people."

Walter Nicgorski

II

As Walter Nicgorski points out, the writers in this book want little to do with the Puritan sense of Americans as a chosen people. Nothing seems more permanently consigned to the past than that literal vision of moral distinction, only to be historically remembered and then with some embarrassment. Even Lincoln's massive, if paradoxical, qualifier, an *almost* chosen people, does little to remove the vast moral arrogance found in the idea, an arrogance all the more intolerable with Vietnam and Watergate still close to mind.

A sense of moral specialness is deeply woven into American history, as many of the writers point out, as is the vision of America as a blessed land in which God's providential design is unfolding. But all of that, the writers say, tells us something about our past, not about our present or our future. Sydney Ahlstrom puts the current response to the Puritan's biblical understanding of being a chosen people very directly: "Then amid the scandals of the 1970's the idea of America as God's New Israel began to be seen as an unfortunate form of national arrogance for all but a minority of chauvinistic reactionaries."

American claims to moral superiority of course linger on in various secularized forms, and especially in the civil-religion formulizations of our social and political thought. Walter Nicgorski also notes that while the contributors to this book reject the Puritan sense of being chosen they are comfortable enough with Lincoln's use of the term to evoke the American experiment in liberty and equality. Thus Peter Berger is willing to suggest that America might still be considered a chosen society in that it is in the vanguard of the world in carrying through the process of modernization while continuing the experiment of free institutions. Martin Diamond makes much the same point. He finds it our "moral mission, so to speak," to teach the world through our political example a correct relationship between equality and democracy.

I want to look at the contemporary mood a bit more by reference to an article by Daniel Bell that seems of a piece with the resistance of the writers gathered here to American moral specialness while yet asserting a limited social and political uniqueness. Bell's remarks, in the bicentennial issue of *Public Interest* referred to by Theodore Hesburgh, are appropriately entitled "The End of American Exceptionalism." The sense of American specialness, he tells us, derived from a view of America as free of the vicissitudes of history, free of the past and free of the laws of development that doomed all human societies to decay and destruction. The special circumstances of the American founding added up to "the idea that, having been 'born free,' America would in the trials of history, get off 'scot free.' " But that was the old notion. "Today," Bell says, "the belief in American exceptionalism has vanished with the end of the empire, the weakening of power, the loss of faith in the nation's future."

American uniqueness was shaped, like any national view, by the experience of nature, religion and history. In each case one can point to special circumstances in America—a vast and abundant land, the Puritan sense of a covenant with God which gave to all actions spiritual significance, and the lack of a feudal past and the opportunity for a fresh start in human affairs. But again, all of that is behind us. Bell writes:

> The United States began with no "history" . . . and for much of its existence as a society its orientation was to the "future," to its Manifest Destiny and mission. Today that sense of destiny has been shattered. Nature and religion have vanished as well. We are a nation like all other nations. . . .

The only remaining "exceptionalism" Bell finds is our history of constitutionalism and the general moral consensus that has accompanied it. This alone, the idea of being a free people with a respect for individual rights and liberties, sets us apart in the world.

Bell's reduced conception of America might seem sharply pessimistic but in fact isn't. The future has indeed receded and we are no longer "the exemplary once-born nation, the land of sky-blue optimism. . . ." But in the confrontation with this loss there remains for us the possibility of "maturity"—that is, the "act of becoming twice-born" through the "recognition of the mortality of countries within the time scales of history." And as we confront our past, with all its gains and losses, with its "moral complexity," we have the opportunity to at least "remain humanized among the nations."

Bell's analysis of American exceptionalism effectively catches the present feeling. We are no longer, if we ever truly were, an exceptional society; at most the only thing that sets us apart in the world is our tradition of constitutional freedom. Yet this isn't a totally disheartening truth about us, for in the recognition of our ordinariness there is the possibility of joining more fully the human community.

Michael Novak, in a recent book called *Choosing Our King*, puts this view most dramatically. We once thought ourselves "entrusted with this planet's fairest dream: a new world, a new Eden. The twentieth would be the 'American century,' during which an almost chosen people would lead mankind to unprecedented moral heights." But it is in the rejection of such adolescent hopes, Novak argues, that it might be said that "the United States is at the threshold of a new maturity, that the nation can, if it wishes, admit into consciousness a sense of its own capacity for evil, an awareness of the tragic quality of life, a respect for limits." In accepting our limits and facing up to our failures we become, at last, a "human nation."

We are hard pressed to resist such a view. The direction of the time in almost all aspects of life urges that we reduce our expectations, put fewer claims upon our national life, expect less. We have, it now seems evident, demanded too much of ourselves, and so we sharply narrow our claims to uniqueness and turn away entirely from our soaring assertions of moral uniqueness. Acutely aware of the misdeeds committed in the name of moral superiority, of being a self-anointed chosen people, we hasten for the "merely" human and point out the virtue in such attainment. Novak, in a recent essay called "In Praise of Cynicism (or) When the Saints Go Marching Out," also tells us that "Morality has always been the nation's fever, unabated, hidden, flaming up. No penicillin has ever penetrated it." The particular cure he offers is a new conception of morality based upon "a gentle cynicism and cultural pessimism." Again, it is hard to resist. There is good reason now for cynicism and pessimism.

Yet nagging questions may remain. Are we, if we assent to the present awareness of moral limitation and take on a gentle cynicism, giving up too much of a national past that has not yet wholly passed away? Is it possible that we become a fully human society only by aiming to be more than that? Is the secularized sense of being a chosen people the only sense in which we can think of ourselves without embarrassment as a special people?

Many analysts of America have pointed to the powerful strain of self-criticism running through our history, in which we acknowledge, often with much pain, the gaps between our ideals and attainments. And since our ideals are almost always expressed in moral terms, the failure to meet them is almost always seen as morally intolerable—perhaps not the wisest way of measuring national success but perhaps not the least effective. Russell Nye, in his book *This Almost Chosen People,* views the national tendency to set high goals and then suffer when they are not met as the necessary movement of moral development in the society:

> Americans therefore must continue to attempt to meet their own high standards, and suffer when they do not; they are no doubt the only people in the world who blame themselves for not having finally created the perfect society, and who submit themselves to persistent self-examination to determine why they have not. Because they have set themselves such an elevated task, they are less willing than others to accept anything less than its accomplishment.

As illustration, Nye points to the nation's long struggle with the legacy of slavery:

> The nation spent nearly a century . . . rationalizing its acceptance . . . fought a bloody war to eliminate it, and has since subjected itself to an agonizing self-appraisal because it has not completely rid itself of the consequences of having once tolerated the system. No other nation has quite the same feelings of guilt over its failures.

Guilt of this sort may be another remaining American "exceptionalism," and a vitally important one. In race relations and other areas of national life it can be a means to health, or at least a spur, an irritation, driving us in that direction. Only a moral people can be truly pained by moral failure. Only belief in a moral past enables us to be truly indignant over an immoral present, for if we were not moral in the past we then cannot have ceased to be moral in the present. If nothing else our extravagant ideals and the accompanying awareness of the failure to secure them provide us with a means of measuring our present situation. They help us locate the place where we have arrived—and where we have yet to go.

Leo Marx in *The Machine in the Garden* has said as much about Jefferson's impossible vision of America as an enduring agrarian republic: "Recognizing that the ideal society . . . was unattainable, he kept it in view as a kind of model, a guide to long-range policies as indispensable to intelligent political thought or action as the recognition of present necessities." Similarly, an ideal vision of America as a moral society, however unattainable the vision may be, provides a kind of model for the continuing reconstruction of an immoral society.

The Puritans saw themselves locked in the moral drama of a chosen people who must either uphold or defile a special covenant with God. The mythic origins of our society are located here, in the hard moral demands placed upon us because of the commensurately great good bestowed on us, in the choice we make between God's blessing or curse. If, in John Winthrop's words, we live up to "the cause between God and us," "we shall find that the God of Israel is among us . . . he shall make us a praise and glory, that men shall say of succeeding plantations: the Lord make it like that of New England. . . ." But if "we shall deal falsely with our God in this work we have undertaken . . . we shall shame the faces of many of God's worthy servants, and cause their prayers to be turned into curses upon us till we be consumed out of the good land whither we are going." The biblical language may be wildly remote from us, but the direct moral vision it embodies may still be widely felt in the land, however shadowy its appearance in current critical thought. And it may still help draw out the best from us, that which is better than we knew was there.

We cannot easily think of ourselves now as a chosen people in the older and explicit religious sense. Even Lincoln's vision of our chosenness as a secularized moral mission has dimmed. As Bell and Novak and many of the writers in this book point out, it is our similarity with other peoples, and especially our moral similarity, that should occupy us now and not our specialness. Surely this is a truth we need to hear. Yet the Puritan heritage of moral specialness is also a truth about us and one that should not be wholly lost sight of however much we feel the pull of current thinking. We don't need our sense of moral superiority reinflated; the dangers here are clear enough. But we may need reminding that the nation has had the highest moral ambitions for itself, has sought to be more than it could and in so doing set moral standards for itself that, however unrealized, are still stirring and perhaps still useful.

Lincoln's wonderfully paradoxical phrase may still tell us something deeply important about ourselves even if we take it in its oldest, unsecularized, and presently unfashionable sense. It still may be the necessary support for all other meanings of the phrase, including its social and political meanings. To be an *almost* chosen people isn't really to be a chosen people at all—but neither is it quite to abandon the notion altogether. This may be the contemporary tightrope we have to walk.

Ronald Weber